Keeping Your Faith In College

Students from over 35 schools across the
country share their experiences living
as a Christian in college

By Abbie Smith

VMI Publishers

Dedication

I could never be grateful enough for the unconditional support from my family and friends throughout this process. I also want to thank the contributors, whose scincere hearts were a constant encouragement to me. Lastly, and by far, most importantly, I humbly thank God for the journey of these past four years, where I realized my life, identity and purpose to be founded in Him. May we never stop living in awe of His glory, broke by His gospel and soaked by His endless flow of grace!

(For more information or to contact Abbie, visit www.keepingyourfaith.com)

Published by VMI Publishers
P.O. Box 1676, Sisters, Oregon 97759

Publisher's note regarding authenticity of the contents of this book:
The stories and experiences you are about to read are drawn from real life situations. In most cases, the names of the colleges have been changed to protect the anonymous nature of this book. These stories come from students who attended one of the actual colleges named. However, in some cases the stories are a compilation of experiences shared by more than one student. The author has personally written or re-written some of the stories in this book.

TABLE OF CONTENTS

PREFACE

Many will tell you college should be the best four years of your life. No parents, no curfews, no getting grounded...basically no rules. In fact, most would sum up college as four years of fraternity parties, football games, late nights leading to hangovers, and maybe a little calculus homework (in case the parents ask). You no longer have a teacher, parent, or other authority controlling your every move. For the first time, you hold the reigns. You make the decisions. And you call the shots. From a religious stand-point, you no longer have your mom dragging you out of bed each Sunday morning for church, or your best friend Johnny knocking on your door for youth group. You're now in a world where beer and boyfriends seem far more impor-tant than beliefs and the Bible.

To put it simply, college is a transition. A huge tran-sition! You are sandwiched between the SAT-focused and often sappy days of high school, and the nebulous future of the real world, where finances become your own and distri-bution requirements are no longer a priority. In a sense, the college years are "in between years," basically providing unlimited ways to indulge yourself. From the world's per-spective, this seems too good to be true, but from a Christian perspective, this can seem pretty scary.

When I began writing this book, I was filled with sheer excitement and enthusiasm. But the more I prayed and thought through it, the more apprehensive I became. "Maybe I had created a good idea, but how was I, a college student and relatively young Christian myself, supposed to write a book for my peers about college life?" Maybe it would make sense if I were a saintly Christian who'd spent my life as a missionary feeding the poor in China. But I'm not. I'm just an average college student challenged to more passionately pursue my walk with Christ every day. I've struggled. I've definitely struggled. And a lot of times I've failed, but the ending to the story remains just as beautiful every time. God cannot help but remain madly in love with the saving grace of Christ in me, regardless of "the me." It is His very nature to *be love* and His heartbeat that we, as His prized creations, would latch on to loving Him.

In writing this book, my eyes have been opened wider to the incredible tendencies and inevitable struggles of being a Christian in college, let alone any stage of life. Similarly, I have realized that a stage is something that serves its purpose for a time. You will reap experience, failure, growth and learning in college that will never again be possible in your life. It's a unique stage of maturity that never will be duplicated. But I'm not going to lie to you; it's a tough stage too. Our faithful Father knew the battles of these years, however, and not only gave Himself and His Word for us, but He also gave us one another. My greatest hope for this book is that it will serve as a sheer encouragement for Christian college students that we are not alone in our faith. I believe that together we'll see that it is, in fact, possible to maintain and more exciting, grow, in our walk as a faithful follower of Jesus Christ throughout the college years.

On the following pages, college students from across the country share their experiences as they have sought to keep their loyalty to God during these years. My prayer is that we will be relieved and refreshed by reading experiences of students who have lived, and are living, in our similar situations. They have had your non-Christian roommate. They have been to that fraternity party. They have had the atheist biology professor. These are stories and experiences of Christians who simply want to discern between what the world wants from their college experience and what God wants from it. This certainly is not to say that the students who contributed to this book have never made mistakes, nor that they have never drifted away from God for a time…quite the contrary. But they have used these times of difficulty and weakness to learn and to strengthen their relationship with their heavenly Father.

    One thing to keep in mind while reading this book is that those sharing their stories haven't had the experience of hindsight. They are still college students. Sometimes it takes God years to reveal what He wants us to learn from a given situation. So be patient with the fact that these stories may reveal only a glimpse of what God intends to teach us about something or someone. And just to make it completely clear, neither myself, nor this book, claim to hold all the answers. It's not going to make you some amazing evangelist on your campus, nor does it devise a plan to lead the entire men's basketball team to Christ. It is simply a compilation of stories to be shared and used, maybe as a guide, or a learning tool, or if nothing else, as a relief that there are other Christians out there struggling, seeking, growing and learning, just like you, during this stage of life.

    With all of that said, I ask you to read and take from this book what you will. Do not see it as a blueprint, or as an approach that must be applied specifically to you or to your campus. These pages share various experiences in various arenas of college life, but I can guarantee that a lot of your experiences will be entirely different. My hope is that you will allow God to use this book as a tool for your life, to show you spiritual truths, which will help strengthen and deepen your personal relationship with Christ. I think one of the reasons there is not a lot of Christian literature focused on this season of life is because people write it off as a time of assumed straying. College students are viewed as a generation of passionate, rebellious and feisty people in a short-lived stage where they're *expected* to mess-up. I'm convinced that this is far from God's agenda, however. College can be an absolutely pivotal and transforming time of growth and maturity in person's life. And specifically for a Christian, by maintaining and even increasing your faith during these years, they can not only be four great years for you, but they can also be four great years for God.

INTRODUCTION

But the fruit of the Spirit is love, joy, peace, patience, kindness, goodness, faithfulness, gentleness and self-control. Against such things there is no law. Those who belong to Christ Jesus have crucified the sinful nature with its passions and desires. Since we live by the Spirit, let us keep in step with the Spirit. Galatians 5:22-25

To say that I've never fallen into temptation while being in college is a pure lie. I am human. I am imperfect. And I am going to be tempted. I hate to break it to you, but you are too. We all are. The way that we react to the temptation, however, is the key. Did you ever look around your campus, classroom, or dorm and say to yourself, you know, this really isn't the way it's "supposed to be." You know what, you're exactly right! God didn't create a culture full of drinking, sex and tight black pants. I mean do you really think that in the Garden, Eve was concerned about what size she wore, or that Adam was worried about his date Friday night? No. That's all stuff that our culture has deemed important and lies that we as humans have bought into.

As Christians, we know deep down that this world doesn't claim *the end*. We have tasted a piece of heaven through knowing God and realize that this span we call life can't be the final destination. Paul voices this in 2 Corinthians 5:2 when he says, "Meanwhile we groan, longing to be clothed with our heavenly dwelling." God created us to be clothed in garments of peace and protection, of beauty and tranquility. And when we truly taste a knowledge of Christ and the beauty of eternity, it becomes more and more difficult to live in a world so far from this picture of paradise; in a world stricken by sin and surrounded by suffering. As Christians, however, we are called to live in this world, yet somehow, not of it.

Do you find it unsettling that you have this amazing love and knowledge of Christ in your life, yet struggle with sharing the truths of the gospel with your roommate? Or are you ever frustrated seeing the lies written all over television, media and the movies, yet so easily sit back and indulge them? We know the falsity of this world and we know the perfect truths of the gospel, but for some reason, it is so difficult to apply this knowledge to our lives. In fact, we'll go to any extreme in an attempt to fill our given void with something other than God, fully knowing from past experience that it leads to nothing but a dead end.

But, and I emphasize this word, but, we are not in heaven yet! We are not, and cannot, be fully "wrapped in the garment of heaven" while we are on earth. And it's utterly clear that this plan was no mistake. 2 Corinthians 5:5 says, "Now it is God who has made us for this very purpose and has given us the Spirit as a deposit, guaranteeing what is to come." Therefore, we who "share in the heavenly calling," should be propelled by nothing less than this "hope offered to us, as an anchor for the soul, firm and secure" (paraphrased Hebrews 3:1, 6:18-19). As Christians, no matter what the circumstances, we are to live on this earth, hopeful of the promises of God given over 4000 years ago. We are to shine our light, our strength and our hope of Christ with those living in darkness. And this is purely so that "you may live a life worthy of the Lord and may please him in every way: bearing fruit in every good work, growing in the knowledge of God, being strengthened with all power according to his glorious might so that you may have great endurance and patience, joyfully giving thanks to the Father, who has qualified you to share in the inheritance of the saints in the kingdom of light" (Colossians 1:10-12). Amen!

Through grace and mercy, God gave us eternity through His precious Son. We know the truth. We know our eternal home awaits us with open arms. God gave us our deposit through the Holy Spirit, but until our time comes, we must be content waiting patiently on the doorstep and fulfilling our role as witnesses and ambassadors for our Savior here on earth. Until the glorious signing day, when Christ will come again, that mansion is not ours. Our house is here on earth. And our faith lies not in relationships, circumstances, or opportunities around us, but in a hope of what we do not see (Hebrews 11:1)...a hope of glory.

I hope this book encourages and helps us to further understand what it means to live happily on this earth, while still knowing and hoping in the paradise that lies beyond. Similarly, to realize the incredible potential of these four years of college...living for God and the amazing mysteries of Him and not for ourselves. And in beginning this book, I think it would be wise to agree upon a portion of this mystery, this love story we refer to as the gospel.

What would you do as an all-powerful god in order to rectify your people from a broken world? Maybe wipe the slate clean, send everyone to heaven and just start with a new race? Better yet, why not just cleanse the hearts of every person on earth and let the world rejoice in harmony? So what was God thinking in taking the seemingly absolute opposite approach by sending Himself, in the likeness of Jesus Christ, as a servant? He came for the very purpose of being persecuted, rejected, hated and ultimately crucified, all for the sake of your life. All for the sake of reconciling humanity. There's no way.

Redemption...unbelievable. Forgiveness; there must have been another way. Love...impossible. The mysterious paradox is, this is exactly what God decided to do. Did it come easily? By no means! It was permeated by pain. Saturated in suffering. And covered in blood. But in God's justice, a sacrifice had to be made. And in His mercy and love, He took that bloody sacrifice upon His own flesh. God did the unthinkable and became the very depths of sin, that we might gain eternal life. Jesus Christ came to endure a life of suffering, meekness, humility and false accusation, in pursuit of one goal: to reclaim the hearts of his children. The sole meaning of the cross is the Creator's unfailing love for His prized creation.

This mystery is depicted throughout the New Testament letters. In a timeless act, Christ chose poverty over riches, merely for the gain of others (2 Corinthians 8:9). And not just a gain of wealth, but also the gain of God's very righteousness, as we are told in 2 Corinthians 5:21. By taking on the likeness of sinful flesh, God did what the presence of human flesh nullified, that of earning God's love and acceptance through following the law.

Thus, the consequences of sin, ultimately leading to death, were nailed and condemned to the cross of Jesus Christ (Romans 8:3). Therefore, the law no longer embodies a form of gaining righteousness before God. "For it is by grace you have been saved, through faith—and this not from yourselves, it is the gift of God—not by works, so that no one can boast" (Ephesians 2:8-9). Christ was crucified that we might be cured. By calling ourselves Christians, we no longer live as sinners enslaved by the law, trying to earn God's love. But we live as sinners willing to admit our helpless condition and need for a Savior, who freed us by the cross and unified us under one new Hope— a hope of glory in Jesus Christ, our Lord. And this, my brothers and sisters, is a glimpse of amazing grace. As my pastor once said, "when a king dies for his subjects, it doesn't say a lot about the subjects. But it says everything about the king." Christ's death was not about us. It was all about God and His infinite glory. For some reason, we have been set apart to serve God on our respective campuses for this stage of our lives. The pursuit is not to figure out what this reasoning is, but rather, to be still before our sovereign God and trust in the knowledge of Him alone. I pray that we can walk this journey together, allowing Christ to teach us what it means not to live for our kingdom, but to live for His.

CHAPTER 1

THE TRANSITION

And my God will meet all your needs according to his glorious riches in Christ Jesus.
Philippians 4:19

You loved your pastor, cherished your youth group, knew everyone in your church and everyone knew you. Life was just getting to that comfortable point, when boom, it was time to pack your bags and leave for college. Isn't this the way the story always seems to go? It's the same one as that summer vacation when on the last day you finally met that cute boy or girl, who turned out to be in your hotel all week long. Better yet, when that spot you worked so hard to earn on the varsity team is dashed when you break your ankle in the first game. These experiences always seem overwhelmingly large and disastrous at the time, but in Gods eye's, they are mere spurts of growth and maturity. Whether it's at church, school, work, or even with friends, our environments are constantly changing and challenging us to evaluate and reevaluate our comfort levels. I believe that these transitions are specific means by which God strengthens us and enables us to better serve Him.

The college transition throws us into a conglomeration of challenging and new environments that will no doubt test and exceed our comfort levels. To make matters harder, college presents endless opportunities, making a mere starting point one of the hardest decisions. How does God expect us to find a ministry, a Bible study, or a church to get involved in, when we can't even find our way to the library? We want to remain faithful in trusting that He has placed us here for a purpose in serving Him, but where do we begin? Where can we possibly find the tools, the energy, or even the time, to do all this? At home, our spiritual lives seemed so much easier and more accessible, whereas in college, it often seems completely confusing and overwhelming. As followers of Christ, we desire to somehow use this time and place for His glory, but how?

It's tempting to think that just because millions of people have successfully made this transition to college, we should be able to as well. Needless to say, fear of admitting that it can be a tough and lonely time takes on the mask of various outlets that are often negative. Our fears manifest themselves on false forms of security and value and essentially, we too often forsake the identity we always knew, in buying into a lie. Loneliness is okay. Fear is understandable. Lack of direction, confusion of purpose, loss of direction—it can all be expected. Maybe a better way to put it is, it *should* be expected. The transition to college should not be taken lightly. It's one of the biggest points of change in our entire lives. The promise, however, is that God knew this and actually planned it. I'm convinced that a purpose in His allowing suffering and times of transition is to once again fix our gaze upon Him; to bring us to our knees in a state of surrender. To once again say Father, "You are the Lord my God, who brought me out of Egypt, out of the land of slavery. I shall have no other gods before you (Exodus 20:2)." You, oh God, are in control.

MY TRANSITION IN BECOMING A CHRISTIAN

EMORY UNIVERSITY

The most impressive time of transition for me wasn't the traditional move off to college after my senior year. I didn't become a follower of Christ until the spring of my freshman year at Emory. This is not to say that I was necessarily "bad" my first year of college, or growing up, but I was walking on no other ground but my own. So my big transition, defined by becoming a Christian, actually didn't come until the beginning of my sophomore year. I never experienced the trauma of leaving a church home, or saying goodbye to close Christian friends. I had the transition of returning to my old friends as a "new" person.

Aside from a battle with anorexia upon entering high school, my days pretty much summed up the poster child of a good life. And actually, throughout high school, this persona only became more developed. I was involved in a number of clubs, played three varsity sports starting my freshman year, was a good student, had great friends and honestly, enjoyed coasting down this river of what I'd been convinced was the perfect life. My senior year climaxed when I was accepted to play tennis at the college of my dreams. Life was good, or so it should have been from the world's eyes.

Upon entering college, however, I was overwhelmed with an uncanny knowledge that something was missing. There was something else I needed. As "happy" as I was, there was still an unquenchable void inside of me. I felt selfish feeling this way, knowing that from the outside, I had everything this world could offer me: a wonderful family, close friends, security, health and certainly happiness. But somehow, I simply wasn't content. Without having a clue as to what it might look like, I knew that something was lacking.

During my freshman year, God showed me that my lack of Him was the basis for my feelings of incompleteness. Though the world provided me with everything it had to offer, that was never going to be "enough." The world would never fulfill me to completion. God showed me that being a Christian wasn't about just believing in a god, or going to church. He displayed to me that it wasn't about following a rule, trying to "be good," or saying a prayer on Thanksgiving. Rather, it was about a relationship with Jesus Christ and living my life for one reason: Him.

So through God's pure grace and the witness of many strong Christians that year, I learned the truth of what living a life for Christ meant. I learned that I could be as "happy" as I wanted, but this happiness would eventually die. It is fleeting, man-made, superficial and most of all, circumstantial. The only eternal happiness I could encounter was through joy. And the only true joy would be through Jesus Christ. As he so simply put it, "I am the bread of life; he who comes to Me shall not hunger, and he who believes in Me shall never thirst" (John 6:35.) No matter what decision, reasoning, or understanding, when we seek His guidance, we cannot go wrong, "For this God is our God for ever and ever, he will be our guide even to the end" (Psalm 48:14).

My transition was hard. I came back to a world of people who didn't necessarily *know* me anymore. However, I've realized that my desire is for this transition to be relived every day. Not in the sense of me being unknown, or misunderstood, or constantly needing to ask for forgiveness. But I want to begin every day of my life, from here on out, resting in the grace of forgiveness that happened on the cross, once and for all. This is freedom. My heart desires a daily transition of crucifying my flesh and bearing witness to life as a new creation. I want to live life under the identity of a new and perfectly glorious name, that of Jesus Christ. My mind has been set upon the things above. My old body of flesh and sin has died and my new life is hidden with Christ in God. And I never have reason to be less than perfectly confident in the pure fact that people I encounter can't help but meet the glory of my Creator, imaged in me (Colossians 3:2-4, 10).

THE FORGING POWER OF MY FRESHMAN YEAR

DUKE UNIVERSITY

I had just finished my junior year of high school. All I could think was, "finally, summer is here. I can sleep in and play golf everyday, this is gonna be great!" My father, however, saw things differently. Not more than a week after exams were done, we were on the road visiting colleges. We must have visited over ten schools within a one-week time span. Every gym started looking the same and every school's statistics began sounding identical. My frustrations came to an abrupt stop, however, when we made our last stop at what turned out to be the school of my dreams—Duke University.

My senior year passed quickly, while acceptance letters arrived and high school graduation came and went. Finally, in late August, I found myself moving into a Duke freshman dorm. I gladly said goodbye to my parents, thrilled with the thought of finally being on my own.

Though it didn't take long for classes and the perils

of college professors to abruptly put a damper on my excitement. I was managing my time with extreme diligence, not wasting a minute, but it still seemed that I would work all day and get nowhere. And although I was studying late into the nights, my grades were poor and I quickly discovered that college wasn't the cakewalk that much of high school had been. On top of that, I wasn't making many friends. It seemed that everyone just want to get drunk and break the all time record for skipped classes. Three weeks into the semester, the 18-year-old who couldn't wait to get out of the house was more homesick than he ever imagined possible.

So there I was, the son of a retired Army officer and a cadet enrolled in Air Force ROTC crying tears of frustration and homesickness almost everyday. I was (and I still am) a very unemotional person, but at that point in my life, I honestly struggled to even walk into the cafeteria without breaking down. I was even more humbled by my inability to call home and not burst into tears while speaking to my father. I had never been so lonely, stressed and unhappy in my life. I reached out for God during that time, and He gave me enough strength to persevere, but the depression stayed. By Thanksgiving, I had already applied to a state school back home, where I could join my old friends in the "fun" of college. I promised my parents that I would seriously pray before making my decision, but in all honesty, I had made up my mind.

One of my biggest struggles during this time was the awareness of my parents' disapproval of my transferring. This devastated me. Although my stubbornness and rebellious nature strengthened my resolve, I was crushed to not have their support. I had sought their approval my entire life. One afternoon during this time, I wrote a song with these lyrics:

Why do rebellion and independence have to be so closely linked?
Why does maturing require desertion from the Army of family?
I have been raised to be released like an arrow from a bow,
Why does that release snap back on his arm as he lets me go?

CHORUS
It seems there is no choice that will end without some pain,
I can go where my heart leads me, and spit in the face of my
name.
Or I can march on, a soldier, to the cadence of command,
Only to wonder what might have been if I had lived as my own
man.

Why can't I see the direction that my hands and feet should go?
Should I follow the path that I see best or follow orders as I was
told?
Will honor be lost if I disobey, and do as I believe?
Will my choice throw mud on a love that could never again be
clean?

Finally, the hurt I felt got the best of me and I confronted them about this angst. They apologized; we made
amends, and then began discussing the pros and cons of my
decision. They kept telling me not to take the "path of least
resistance." To me, that wasn't the issue. If one path had
less resistance, that meant I could do more for myself and
more for God. Then my dad asked me a question that I will
never forget, "Where in the Bible did God ever tell anyone
to take the easier way? It was always the harder way." I
paused and realized he was right, but immediately thought
of several reasons why that did not apply to me. About two
seconds later, before I ever spoke, the conviction of the
Holy Spirit rushed upon me like the weight of the ocean. I
found myself laying face down on the floor, sobbing with

the realization that he was right. God *did* want me to take the harder way, and I was to return to Duke. I was not going to "live as my own man." I was going to live as God's man. In that moment, I felt a closeness with both my Heavenly Father and my earthly father that I will never forget. It was the perfect picture of God calling His people to perseverance, while providing the strength and comfort to achieve it.

Upon returning to Duke, I was still scared. It took only a few hours, however, to completely feel God's peace and reassurance in my life; and only a few days to see the amazing evidence of God's promise. I ended up joining a fraternity and enjoying many new friendships, as well as witnessing opportunities that I never dreamed possible. As for the academics, they were still tough, though I managed to adjust and reprioritize my workload. I was also asked to join the Leadership Team for the Fellowship of Christian Athletes. The members of that team, as well as the rest of FCA, have turned out to be my closest friends.

My time at Duke has been the most challenging time of my life, but by far the most rewarding. The wisdom and maturity I have gained from the horrors of my freshman year have strengthened my faith in more ways than I can count. Whether in high school, college, or even the infamous "real world," honoring God and pursuing His direction will open doors of blessing that you would have never thought possible. As Paul says in Romans 8:28, "And we know that in all things God works for the good of those who love him, who have been called according to his purpose." Though the packages may come in different shapes and sizes, God loves to shower His blessings upon us. Some gifts will be more tedious or time-consuming to unwrap, but the fact of the matter is, just as a loving Father longs to bless his children, so our Heavenly Father longs to bless us.

Regardless of what our carnal eyes may perceive, may we each have eyes to see the rich blessings of God being poured upon our lives today.

OVERCOMING TEMPTATION

PENN STATE

Transitioning into college was one of ease and over-whelming obstacles. On the one hand, there was nothing better than leaving home to the unknown freedoms of complete independence. But on the other hand, as some of you may know and the rest are soon to find out, the college years can certainly be confusing. Like many of us, I grew up in the church, constantly surrounded by Christians. Going to church and participating in every youth activity has been second nature to me since preschool. I came from a loving family and have always been certain of my place in God's kingdom. However, something changed when it was time for me to head off to college.

I attended a hometown college, so there were no goodbyes to the family or church congregation. I didn't have to adjust to a new city, or a different culture, for it was already in place. So my initial transition into college was the easy part. My strong foundation, however, still didn't prevent me from encountering the daily temptations virtually every college student faces. All-night clubs and parties, drinking, sex and so forth, all of a sudden found themselves waiting on my doorstep. Decisions of whether, or not, to let them creep into my path was no easy feat. In spite of being a Christian since age 11, for the first time I started questioning the most basic elements of Christianity and why I wanted to live for God. He would still love and accept me, even if I stray for a little while, right?

Wrestling with the temptations of constant knocks on my door became part of a process I grappled with my entire freshman year. All year I went through the motions of being a "bare minimum Christian." In my mind, I had assured myself of a place in God's kingdom. I went to church every Sunday, Bible Study on Wednesday, and participated in the college ministry activities. I was doing what I was accustomed to, but amidst all the temptations that faced me daily, the question of needing an intimate relationship with my Creator was left lingering. I wanted to have sex, I wanted to go to parties and drink, to listen to degrading music with immoral lyrics, and I wanted to watch violent and romantically deceiving movies. Simply put, I wanted to be like every other normal college student in the world. But I can say with thanksgiving now, God had a different idea in mind.

Through His word and through His people, He began to reveal a plan to me, not only for the body of Christians, but specifically for me. He began to answer my question-"Why can't I be like every other college student?" I was led to the following passage in 1 Peter 2:9 which reads, "But you are a chosen people, a royal priesthood, a holy nation, a people belonging to God, that you may declare the praises of him who called you out of darkness into His wonderful light." Wow! This one verse contains so much and I could go on for days digging through its meaning. Two specific points stand out to me.

First, God tells us who we are. In the search for understanding our purpose in life, it is so important to know who we are and more importantly, who we are in Christ. Knowing this allows us to realize our identity on this earth, thus propelling our lives towards a given purpose. This verse reveals that once we are saved, we are a chosen people, a royal priesthood, a holy nation, a people belonging to God. For me, this means that I no longer belong to this earthly, secular world of drugs, drinking, sex, and immorality, but I belong to God—the holy and righteous Creator of the universe. I have been set apart from this world and have joined God's royal family. Second, as if this weren't enough, He goes on to tell us our purpose, once we are saved: to declare the praises of the one who brought you out of darkness into the wonderful light. This light was Jesus. He brought me out of the darkness that this world had cast upon me. And because of His sacrifice, I am now able to sing His praises to all and share the wonderful news that He freely offers to each one of us.

Once I began to wrap my heart around these concepts, I was able to realize my purpose on campus. My glorification of God comes in being devoted to seeking and sharing His love to all who need Him. And this is exactly what Jesus commanded His disciples to do: "Therefore go and make disciples of all nations, baptizing them in the name of the Father and of the Son and the Holy Spirit" (Matthew 28:19). I'm by no means saying I'm perfect, or that I have successfully warded off all temptations that linger upon my doorstep. Every day is full of mercy and grace, and as I seek God and an intimate relationship with Him alone, I only long to know the sound of His knock more clearly. Although I will inevitably continue to stumble, I won't fall; although my vision may become blurry, I won't lose sight; and although at times I may desire to reject His plan, I'll know that God's plans for me will never go silent.

DEFINING MY FOUNDATION

CORNELL UNIVERSITY

Being the first time I've ever been separated from the support of my parents, my initial days at college have been very difficult. They have challenged my self-worth and confidence in a powerful way. My parents were my constant reassurance, always encouraging my capabilities and strengths, even when I failed. Thus, a big struggle for me has been deciding where to find my worth. For the first time, the stable house that I thought embodied the entirety of my worth is gone (or has moved places). I need to figure out how this time around, I can find a more stable worth in which to put my hope.

A house that lasts is built upon a good foundation. When I went to college, the first thing I lost was a grasp of my true foundation. At birth, we are dealt a hand that we have no reason, or really ability, to question. I've realized in these last two years that to have true life, God must be your base. He is the beginning of my assumptions, of every-thing I can know and understand. I will never comprehend the fullness of God's mind, though thankfully, my existence was never pending upon my understanding of God. To say otherwise would negate reason, for reason itself depends on a universal authority. I am a creature, not God. So as Paul explains it in Romans 9 and God himself says at the end of the book of Job, "who am I to question God?"

Flowing from God are the gospel, the Bible, and the source of meaning, stability and success. Because God is the beginning of knowledge, to know and understand is to surrender to and trust Him. This truth is encompassed in the gospel: I am hopelessly lost in myself but can be wholly in submission to the God of the universe. By affirming this truth, we never make ourselves righteous. The gospel destroys pride and arrogance as well as self-loathing and insecurity. I've learned that the Bible is not true because it makes sense, for that would mean we'd be submitting to our autonomous minds, and a mind in rebellion will never admit it is true. Though God's Word makes sense when you examine it, it is not subject to sense and reason; it is the basis for it. This is the ground on which true life is built. Out of surrendering to God and His Word flow meaning, stability and success. The most any of us wants out of life is true happiness and constant joy flowing from a deep sense of meaning, which lets us know our life amounts to something. During college, God has taught me and certainly continues to teach me, that through the God of Abraham, Isaac, Israel and the Bible in its entirety, this is possible.

Once I recognized the gospel as the foundation of God, I also recognized my part in God's big plan. In seeking His kingdom and righteousness, I saw that I had a false impression of my worth being based on the fleeting, temporal world of earthly success, which naturally left me unfulfilled. Instead, I found a cause worth fighting, living, and dying for, that which can never be tarnished or destroyed. This discovery since transitioning to college has given me purpose and meaning, because I see now that everything I do is part of The Ultimate Plan, not my temporal one. Likewise, I have stability because, well frankly, God is truth and to live stably in His universe, I needed to start by accepting His righteousness as my foundation.

WAIT LISTED

BOSTON UNIVERSITY

My college decision was far from what I expected. As my senior year of high school approached, I remember caring about one application and one application only— University of Notre Dame. My entire family had gone there, I lived nearby and I loved the school spirit. Everything fit perfectly. There were a million and one reasons why I knew this school had practically been built for me. Application submissions came and went and by the end of my senior year, I had received acceptance letters from every school, except one. Notre Dame had placed me on a waiting list. I was in shock. I questioned whether God played any role in my college decision and if so, why would He make me sit in torture for the next three months (before I would finally be admitted to Notre Dame)? Did He not care about my desires, my dreams and my obvious destiny to be at that school?

Understanding the difference in God's desires and in our desires isn't exactly a simple thing. For the first time in my life, I was forced to sit back and trust God, waiting patiently for the next letter. I knew patience wasn't always my best quality, so I was reluctantly thankful that He was teaching me this. The months passed and I finally received the much-anticipated letter from Notre Dame. The opening line read, "We regret to inform that you will not be a part of this year's freshman class." I was lost. How had God not realized that this was what was best for me? I felt totally let down and questioned God's decision, let alone existence.

Come fall, I was one of the last to leave for school, let alone, the only one leaving for a second choice school.

My loneliness and dread of attending a second choice school only made matters worse. Transferring after first semester loomed as a strong possibility. When move-in day finally arrived, however, I was pleasantly surprised. My roommate was so sweet and my dorm was beautiful. I came to realize that there were many other people in my same position. After the first month of school, I was even happily involved in one of the campus ministries. God was daily revealing to me the very reasons He put me on this campus and had surrounded me with specific followers of Christ, who completely spurred and encouraged my spiritual growth.

I'm sure Notre Dame would have been a lot of fun and certainly an enjoyable four years. I see know, however, that going to Notre Dame would have kept me in my comfort zone. My old friends would have been down the hall, my family would have been a car ride away and essentially, there would have been no overt challenges to where I was at that point in my life. From day one at Boston University, I have been faced with new challenges in various arenas of my life, most importantly, my walk with God. Every day, I see more and more clearly God's reasoning in placing me on this campus, where His light longs to be seen.

THE CURVEBALL

UNIVERSITY OF ILLINOIS

I have always been very thankful for my family. Even as a child, I consistently thanked God for the family I had and assumed that it would always be a stable force in my life. Then two weeks before I left for college, my parents sat us down and told us they were separating. This caught me completely off guard. My brother and I were expecting the, "with Todd going away to college, we're really gonna have to watch our finances" speech. Instead we received the biggest curveball of our entire lives. My dad gave everything the sense of being temporary, but I think we all knew none of this was going to be short-lived. On that day, both my brother and I realized that the foundation of security we had grown up with was beginning to deteriorate beneath our feet.

Very shaken by the news, I left immediately and went over to a good friend's house. While I tried to hold back the tears, I failed miserably. My poor brother didn't have a friend nearby and obviously didn't have an outlet to go to within the house. This made those final weeks before leaving for school some of the most awkward and difficult days of my life. On the surface, nothing had necessarily changed around the house, but we all knew the truth behind what was going on.

I was finally able to leave for school and temporarily forget what was going on at home. The biggest challenge for me was to accept all of this as a reality that wasn't going to change. The only thing I could and can do to continue my healing is to face the facts head-on. This is not a nightmare that I can wake-up and erase, but it's a living part of my reality. Another huge challenge was learning to accept my mother and father for who they were. Unfortunately, my parents battle the same sins that I do every day. It is hard to come to grips with the fact that your parents have weaknesses and imperfections and come from the same broken race you do.

During my junior year in college I finally began seeing a counselor who helped me externalize some of my thoughts. While I despised the idea of seeing a counselor, the encouragement of a few close friends to do so was such a blessing. I clearly needed guidance on the healing process, let alone a willing ear to listen.

That same year another curve ball was thrown at me when my father remarried. Not only that, but at the wedding, he announced the pregnancy of his new wife. I have had a lot to take in these past few years and realize that the complete restoration and learning process of these events is far from complete. But in an unusual way, these circumstances have brought me closer to God. In short, it was easy for me to remain comfortable when my family was intact, but my need and dependency on God became much more apparent when this comfort was taken away. Living comfortably is a gift that should never be taken for granted, but the realization and preparation that uncomfortable days may come is similarly important.

In writing all of this, I am by no means saying that divorce, in and of itself, is good or will always have a positive impact on the people involved. I have struggled horribly with many things that would never have been an issue had my life not been influenced by a broken home. I've realized that my greatest struggles are almost always rooted in some sort of seed resulting from my parent's divorce. Thankfully though, God, through Christ, has supremacy over everything, and therefore He alone serves as my refuge of strength and unfailing comfort. As Saint Augustine wrote, "God is so powerful that he can create good out of evil." In the same way, while the impact of divorce on one's life would seem totally negative, through God's awesome power, He can use it for good.

CHAPTER 2

THE ACADEMIC LIFE

The earth is the Lord's, and everything in it.
1 Corinthians 10:26

From a worldly perspective, college is a time to enrich your understanding of life through various arenas of study and new environments. From a Christian perspective, there is one subtle difference, an added bonus if you will. We have the opportunity to gain all the academic and relational knowledge, but we've also been blessed with a mission field to share and spread the love of Jesus Christ to thousands of students from around the world! Many peers we sit by in class, in the dining hall, or even while working out in the gym, have never had the opportunity to hear the amazing gospel message of Christ. They don't know the amazing story of God's grace, who by sending His only son to die on a Roman cross, bridged the gap of humanity's fallenness and invited all to join in the most adventurous love relationship ever!

I realize and even delight in my opportunity to share God's love during these years, but I still tend to have incredibly selfish ambitions about college. It's far too easy to have the idea that college is plainly for me, for my benefit and gain. It's for my education, my growth as an individual, my clubs, my meetings, my sports, my parties and on and on and on. Knowing how much there is for me at school and how easily my desires can be fulfilled, often makes focusing on God that much harder. I think two of His most useful gifts pertinent to this topic are discernment and time management. Now, whether we tap into these gifts is another story!

Although there are infinite things college offers each one of us, and I think God wants us to profit from many of them, we must also remember the ultimate purpose in our being here. Is it for us, or for Him? A constant lesson God has taught me throughout college, often through failure, has been about prioritizing my time. First and foremost must be my daily time with Him. After that, rest, studying and fellowship with both believers and non-believers aim to comprise the majority of my days. By realizing that my priorities for God must come first, the things that once seemed disordered take on a new perspective and practically fall into place.   By better prioritizing my time and energy on God's agenda, I am better able to discern between His plans for my life and this campus, versus mine.

Academics are no exception. We are clearly at college to learn and I refuse to doubt that God desires to use every last page you read and seminar you attend for His glory and growth in your heart. But how often do we struggle to understand our purpose in an introductory French class? And does God really care if we wake up for our 8:30 a.m. biology lab? These questions of good stewardship are universal and challenge students across the country. The battle leaves no room for denying the truth, however, "For my thoughts are not your thoughts, neither are your ways my ways," declares the Lord (Isaiah 55:8). I pray that this generation of college students would somehow embrace the gift of our intellect and ability to grow mindfully during these four years. That we would increase our capacity to understand, know and effectively testify to the witness of God's story, ultimately declaring His name to the ends of the earth.

MY ULTERIOR MOTIVE

NEW YORK UNIVERSITY

Before coming to NYU, I made it very clear to my parents and friends that the sole purpose in my going to college was witnessing to outsiders. College was going to be far more about spreading the gospel to my peers, than it was about learning in the classroom. And I was convinced that God could have no other agenda than this. However, I quickly learned that His plans for me during these years were a little different. Within the first month of my arrival, He began revealing to me the great importance of academics. Somehow I had spent my entire life overlooking the final word of what Jesus claimed as the greatest commandment: "Love the Lord your God with all your heart, and with all your soul and with all your mind" (Matthew 22:37).

God has blessed me with an ability to learn and to gain wisdom through my intellect. Why would He want me to neglect it? We are commanded to love the Lord with all of our mind, which at this stage of our lives, means committing to learning all that He would have for us in college. When we study, we are loving God, not to mention developing our minds so that we are better equipped to effectively minister to others! "Therefore, prepare your minds for action…" (Peter 1:13). The value that God places on using our minds is clear, and knowing how important learning is to Him has provided me with more than enough motivation to get the most out of my college academics.

THE CLASS THING

EMORY UNIVERSITY

I was out to dinner with my dad about one month into my freshman year. As you can imagine, the first month had been extremely busy with orientation (which always seems rather disorienting), staying in touch with old friends, meeting new friends, getting settled in my room and changing my schedule. After explaining all my news about tennis, Emory Christian Fellowship, College Ministry and my discipleship group, my dad finally asked me, "Well that's great sweetheart, but are you by any chance taking any classes (i.e. the thing I keep writing checks for)?"

Wow, I continually have to bring this question to my mind while being at school. It sounds crazy, but it's truly far too easy to get wrapped up in various clubs, activities and even Bible studies or ministries, that we forget one of the biggest purposes in our being at college in the first place— to learn. Not to mention that fact that skipping classes becomes as habitual as taking a shower for most students. We won't even start to try and defend that one biblically! God wouldn't have blessed us financially, or intellectually, to attend our respective schools if He didn't want us to learn something there. Yes, it is safe to say that a lot of our learning comes from places other than the classroom, but at the same time, we cannot neglect the knowledge available to us in this setting. Education is a beautiful thing ordained by God. Take advantage of these four years of spiritual growth, but also of intellectual growth. I'm tempted to confine academics to the classroom, or even to a school setting, but who knows how God may someday choose to use your education!

MY PEACE IN CONFUSION

UNIVERSITY OF GEORGIA

I came to college having absolutely no idea what I wanted to do in life. I figured it would become clear after experimenting with some classes and finding a field suited to my interests. Well, I have some daunting news; I'm going into my third year of school and still have absolutely no idea! One afternoon, while I was beginning to get a bit stressed about this notion, God faithfully directed me to Proverbs 16:9 which reads, "In his heart a man plans his course, but the LORD determines his steps." What peace I felt in realizing that no matter how much my parents, friends, professors, or even conscience, nag me about determining my precise direction in life, God is ultimately in control of my every step! What could be more comforting and more encouraging in terms of my perspective in college?

We have heard that "faith can move a mountain," but until recently, I thought this was just pretty "New Testament talk," with a little nature imagery thrown in for spice. During these years of college, however, God has shown me otherwise. Whenever I struggle with maintaining perspective on the burdens or confusions of life, in other words the "mountains," I am quick to question God's intervening power. Does He actually care that I'm battling like this? Does He understand how this is affecting my relationships and even my every day walk with Him? In response to my doubts, God never ceases to remind me that it is in times like this, that our faith allows us to look past these mountains and into His precious gaze. For when we look to God, it is no longer a mountain that comes into focus, but a fading hill. I've learned the hard truth in college that time is often the best cure in a given situation. Because with time, God grants us the ability to gain new perspective on our mountains and turn them into mere hills of hope.

So although I still have no idea where my career path will lead me, or even what that career path will be, God is teaching me, more and more each day, to trust in His steps and His promises. He longs to be the step-by-step tour guide over the hills of my life. And I know that maintaining this trust will allow my perspectives, on a daily and a long-term basis, to be so much clearer!

DON'T BE AFRAID TO SPEAK UP

WASHINGTON UNIVERSITY

Environmental science was a distribution require-ment that I hope to never be tested on again. On the same note, however, God somehow used this class to teach me a mighty lesson. Early one Tuesday morning, the teacher was lecturing on the idea that "plate tectonics" was the cause for everything in existence. A friend sitting next to me some-what jokingly said, "Oh really, did Jesus just appear out of the rocks?" Those around us chuckled a bit and even our professor put on a sort of half-grin. He went on, however, to explain that not only the creation of earth, but also all interactions, relationships, objects, and even emotions on earth, point back to this theory of plate tectonics. Now I'm not trying to bash science, or plate tectonics (well...), but I definitely have faith that God is the reason for our existence and life, rather than a spontaneous collision of the earth's plates. This is not to say that science and religion can't co-exist. Quite the contrary. But my professor was claiming that plate tectonics can exist alone and is in fact the reason for the evolution of religion. Who knows? Maybe God ordained the whole plate tectonics and big bang stuff? But regardless, I believe in a God who not only creates, but also orchestrates.

Now getting back to Tuesday morning, my friend boldly raised his hand and spoke out about his beliefs. By being honest with his convictions, he not only reminded our professor about being objective in his teachings, but he also made a statement to the class about his beliefs as a Christian. My friend wasn't fazed by the professor's title or his position. He was fazed by the fact that Christ did something for us 2000 years ago that simply can't be overlooked today. As disciples of Christ, it is our job not to be ashamed or intimidated by the lies and falsehoods that will inevitably exist around us. This isn't easy and honestly I don't know if it ever will be (you didn't see me speaking up when the professor taught these theories). I just hope that when each of us is faced with threats, intimidated by an authority, conversation, or even a friend, we do not flee, but trust the Lord to give us boldness and allow His blessings to flourish.

CHARACTER VERSUS CAREER

FURMAN UNIVERSITY

It's hard not to be consumed by career paths and "life in the real world," during this season of life. Many would say we're in school for this very reason, to get a job afterward. And probably more would say that the school we attend, our cumulative GPA, or even our lengthy resume, are what ultimately constitute our professional success. I'm not here to bash college as a preparatory tool, or even to discourage it's impact on our future, but I do think it's far too easy to view these years as the "end all" in terms of our future hopes. This stems back to flawed perspectives thrown at us by parents, professors, media and even the American culture. I'm not convinced, however, that the commonly held perspective of college, or professional life for that matter, is necessarily correct.

We all know rich, happy people and we all know rich, unhappy people. Similarly, we all know not so rich, happy people and not so rich, unhappy people. Point being, money and the world's definition of success doesn't always have a happy ending. As this relates to us, graduating first in your class, or with the longest list on your resumé, doesn't guarantee happiness. If we can all agree that this is the case, then why does God want us in college? Well, I'm convinced that He has incredible purpose and potential for these years; essentially God is not necessarily fixated on the days to come, as much as the days of present. I think our Father in heaven wants more for us out of these years, than our finite minds could ever imagine. I also think, however, that His desires for us in college relate more to our character potential at present, than for our career paths down the road.

Imagine that you were to die tomorrow. What would you want to be remembered for... good grades, a solid list of contacts, highest honors in your major? Or would it be things about your character...honesty, purity, Godliness, wisdom, patience? What I'm trying to say is this, many things we wrap our daily time and energies around will soon waste away like vapor. But other things will impact and remain invested in people eternally. Which of these is more appealing?

For me, it's obvious and simply a matter of asking what in my life is going to pass away, regardless of the six-digit income it may contribute to this lifetime. And what in my life needs to be prioritized as an eternally impactful investment? From a practical standpoint, I haven't stopped studying, or started skipping classes to further my character development, but I have tried to be more cognizant of the importance of relationships and personal growth. I truly believe that if I can get my moral and relational values more aligned with God's, than He's got more than enough in store for my needs professionally.

LEARNING TO STAND

GORDON COLLEGE

The trumpet call of my alarm clock sounded a shrill battle cry. Tense and alert, I sat straight up in bed, clutching my graphite weaponry in hand. I looked down and saw crumpled loose-leaf pages, along with sharpened pencils, which had left smudge marks on my sheets overnight. I rubbed my dry eyes and crawled out of bed to dull attention. All around me were opened books, unfinished paragraphs, and website references. I, a new cadet involuntarily con-scripted into the army of literature, was suffering some seri-ous battle wounds.

Let me start from the beginning. I walked into my freshman poetry seminar on a regular Thursday afternoon ready to commence my academic training. I had my neces-sary reserves. I had even brought notes from my high school Advanced Placement English classes to give me the edge on my fellow soldiers of education. I was armed, I was ready, I was fired up and prepared to jump the hurdles of grammar, climb the ropes of creative thinking, and target the concept of active reading. There was even the occasional class session when I would heed instructions behind an overturned desk, crouched and listening for the call of William Shakespeare himself. Poetry was my passion, the one subject in school worth fighting for. I would fall on my sword for a sonnet by John Keats, and I was certain my valiant efforts would in turn produce medals of honor for my numerous ideas.

Well, there comes a day when every good soldier is sent to the home front, and this particular Thursday was my call. Our poetry professor assigned us our first paper, and like any other giddy new recruit, I was anxious to make him proud. For the next few days I enlisted myself into solitary confinement. I stayed in my dorm room, eyes glued to my computer, reciting poems and looking up data in an attempt to compare modern poetry with styles of the past. Writing essays about comparing works of literature was my strongest skill! I poured my soul into that paper, pulling out all the knowledge I had ever gained about composition. When I handed my superior those precious four pages of basic training put into action, I was sure he would be just as proud of my work as I was.

The next time we had our morning call to order, my professor explained that he wanted to conference with us individually about our papers. His tone of voice sounded resigned and negative, but I assumed he was talking to the rest of class. Surely he couldn't be referring to my master-piece! I smiled to myself. I knew that paper was a tank, and nothing could touch it.

As it turns out, the paper was not a tank. The truth is, it wasn't even a bow and arrow. My English professor tore that essay apart like a foreign spy with highly classified information. As I walked out of his office after our conference, I felt the tears fall like nuclear bombs mushrooming my sadness on the sidewalk. Although a good fighter never cries, I couldn't hold back my disappointment. A huge part of my soul was in that paper, so it was more than getting a bad grade. I felt like I had failed as a cadet, and I began to question whether I even belonged in college at all. Could I handle it? Would I ever have what it takes to succeed? Was I good enough?

Which brings us to the next morning, when I woke up groggy and in a whirlwind of emotions. My confidence had been severed, and I was faced with a huge decision. I was either going to continue my training, or accept my emotional stalemate and go back home. Standing there in my room with remnants of my failed paper all about me, I wondered how my schoolwork related to my relationship with God. From an eternal perspective, one paper doesn't seem so huge, but why did I feel so defeated?

I began to think about my life as a child of the Lord. Essentially, my role on this earth is for the glorification of my Father in heaven. I realized that I was approaching my school assignments for myself, desiring to highlight my own talents, and essentially to earn affirmation and praise. I began to picture what it would be like if my goal in every homework assignment was to glorify God. More so, imagine if I fully understood my worth in Christ's eyes, rather than the eye's of the university faculty, my parents, or even my peers. What if I had been able to receive that constructive criticism with joy, realizing that the conference with my teacher was a gift from God? It was a prime witnessing opportunity for me to show maturity and grace, rather than having portrayed a defensive attitude about my work. These thoughts flooded my mind as I imagined myself fighting through the battle of higher education, working and striving toward an ultimate victory. I realized that my goal had to be merely equipping myself with the tools God had given me. Christ was the only one capable of arming me for the challenges in my life, even for something as small as a poetry paper.

In retrospect, I see how the Lord has changed my heart about schoolwork. I have since learned many valuable lessons from my English professor's advice, and have re-centered my focus on the sweet face of Christ. I am slowly learning to allow the Lord to ready me for battle, desiring my efforts to be pleasing to Him alone. Although college can seem huge, overwhelming, and stressful at times, I remember where my strength comes from. So "Finally, be strong in the Lord and in his mighty power...Therefore put on the full armor of God, so that when the day of evil comes, you may be able to stand your ground, and after you have done everything, to stand" (Ephesians 6:10 and 13).

CHAPTER 3

DORM LIFE

The Lord will fulfill his purpose for me;
Your love, O LORD, endures forever—
do not abandon the works of your hands.
Psalm 138:8

I'm convinced that living with others is one of the best ways for them to see your relationship with Christ, let alone one of the most challenging means of accountability for your faith. However, it's also one of the most challenging forms of witness you will ever have. A roommate sees you on rainy days, sunny days, good days, bad days, busy nights and boring nights. There's no hiding behind closed doors when your roommate shares those doors with you. St. Francis of Assisi writes an encouraging note on this by saying, "Share the gospel at all times and when necessary, use words."

College dorms must claim one of the most plentiful harvests, though as timid as we are to admit it, with some of the fewest workers. It's challenging to make a bold statement in front of this environment of people, because they can hold you accountable to every last move you make. It's no longer the group you can say one thing to Sunday morning and then hide from the remainder of the week. Nor is it your eight a.m. to four p.m. school friends, your four thirty to six thirty p.m. sports friends, or your seven to nine p.m. youth group. These people live with you around the clock. Therefore, making the claim to be a Christian sets you up for the most challenging and sometimes humiliating accountability ever!

Nonetheless, you are in a unique stage of life where God is allowing you to live amongst the masses, to live in an environment you will most likely never again experience through your entire lives. Yes, dorm life can be exhausting. Yes, the loud music, profanity, late hours, drunken bouts at three a.m. and even the additional sleeping guest in your room can throw some windy curve balls in your expectations of a living arrangement. But at the same time, Christ is giving us an unbelievable opportunity to share where the sharing is needed most. You have opportunities to share in the midst of struggle, confusion, doubt and sheer disgust in your surroundings. The love of Christ is the most powerful weapon known to man. May each of us embrace its capacity and desire to let it reign through our lives and specifically in our living situations throughout these years.

NOT ME

TEMPLE UNIVERSITY

God blessed me with three wonderful roommates my sophomore year. Throughout the summer I prayed that I would be able to share my faith and witness to them in the clearest way possible. I knew that my faith had grown immensely that summer and I wanted to be sure they could see the changes. Throughout the year, however, God allowed me to realize two very important things.

First, I didn't need to set up, or schedule, any of these "God-talks." Though I did need to pray expectantly and seek to be prepared for them, God would make them happen in His timing. They would happen if my walk was happening. Even on my most organized day, I could have never planned all the conversations and impromptu questions that came my way about Christianity. Why do I get up early to read the Bible? Why don't I drink? Do I ever get mad at people? How can I be so confident in something I can't prove? Wow! What fun questions, which are so bold for my roommates to ask, but also so challenging for me to answer! So it was actually the wisdom and words I needed to be praying for, not the when's or where's.

Secondly, I realized that two of the most impactful aspects of someone's Christian walk are steadiness and passion. When anyone sees a person living an alternative lifestyle or possessing a great passion for something, it inevitably sparks curiosity. If we, as Christians, do all that we can to reflect God's light, then He will surprise us and in turn do all that we cannot, and more.

A clear highlight of college, let alone my life, happened that sophomore year. Late one night over a take-out Chinese dinner, one of my roommates finally laid it out that she knew I was different and that all my Christian friends were too. Unable to put a finger on what it was exactly, she wanted to know how and why we were different and if I thought she could ever "do it." After an amazing conversation of talking through how it was never going to be about what she or I could do, but about what Christ had done, my roommate prayerfully accepted the love of her Savior and the acknowledgement of His freedom granted to her on the cross that night.

I know this seems like the textbook story that we all pray for, though think will never happen to us, but honestly, it did. All I had done was try to live a life glorifying to God and His teaching, and as promised, He took care of the rest. God planted a seed of curiosity and courage in my roommate's heart, which resulted in our study of the Gospel of John. This eventually led to weekly Bible study on my hall. How fun is God! So, although our timing is often a little different than His, be patient, for those around you cannot help but see Christ in and through you when you're abiding in Him.

DAILY SEEDS

NEW YORK UNIVERSITY

For months before going away to school, I consistently prayed for my soon-to-be roommates. I had no idea what to expect, but was excited when God provided me with two, conservative, "good girls." Although both had been raised in religious families, the personal nature of God and His daily role in our lives was a total mystery to them. I found that one of the most powerful things I could do was to simply share with them the Lord's everyday blessings in my life.

I started out by intentionally writing prayer requests, or various ways I desired for the Lord to bless my opportunities or circumstances on a given day, on a posted white board. At first I think they viewed it as some weird habit their psycho-Christian roommate needed to take comfort in. As the year progressed, however, they began to expect and even be curious about seeing how the Lord had been faithful to me, according to what I had written on the board. They would sometimes ask me the specifics of something I wrote, or even about the progress of something that had been posted the previous week. It wasn't long before they started recognizing God's faithfulness to His promises and how excited He is to answer our prayer requests. Similarly, they began to notice God's blessings in their own lives, and therefore His personal presence available to each of them. We were able to talk about the difference in the "try your hardest to be a good person" life and the "life lived in surrender to the Savior." And this, of course, led to conversations about the differences in religion and doctrines, versus the freedom of the gospel and God's grace.

As my roommates continue to experience God's realness and desire to be intimately part of their lives, I can only trust God's words that, "He who began a good work in you will carry it to completion until the day of Christ Jesus" (Philippians 1:6).

I WANT TO BE SPENT

ELON UNIVERSITY

Jesus was gladly spent for Paul and thus Paul says that he is gladly spent for the sake of the Corinthians (2 Corinthians 12:15). In fact, the writer of Hebrews goes so far as to claim that, "it was fitting that God, for whom and through whom everything exists, should make the author of their salvation perfect through suffering" (Hebrews 2:10). As a Christian, I am a minister of Christ's love to those who do not know Him. That means being spent for their sake. After realizing the love God has for me and how spent He was in the pursuit of my heart, I can be joyously spent for others. And I am humbled in knowing that I am not doing this alone, but in a co-working relationship with the God of creation!

School has been my obsession. I am very driven. My constant temptation is to bury myself in homework, in order to fulfill my academic expectations. But God wants my time directed toward a far better end—toward an eternal end. One evening, one of my hall mates and I were talking and she explained how much she longed for the love of a man, having never experienced that love from her father. I dumbly listened, and missed the perfect opportunity to tell her of the love of God. That night, realizing the opportunity missed, I cried myself to sleep as I prayed that God would give me another chance to tell this precious girl about God's perfect and all-sufficient love for her.

The next night I went to church, despite having a ten-page paper due the next morning that I had yet to start. I couldn't escape the conviction that God wanted me to go. After the sermon, a random student got up and explained that he thought God just wanted the congregation to be reminded of His love. He explained God's love in such a profound way, that my heart and mind were literally giddy for the rest of the night. So much so that upon arriving home, my roommate couldn't help but ask what had happened at church. I was able to explain to her that God had freshly reminded me about the love of God. That was one of the first times I'd tangibly realized the joy derived from obedience. God also used it to remind me that regardless of where I am, or how fruitless I seem to be, He is endlessly watching over my life. Exhausted and with no paper in hand, I went to sleep, entrusting my paper to God. I kid you not – I woke the next morning having dreamt the plans for the paper. I had a lot of writing assignments that semester, but this one was by far the best.

I was not without fault after learning these immense and all-sufficient truths about God's love. And to my knowledge, my hall mate did not become a Christian that term. But God has so much more for us than just winning a battle against sin, or witnessing so that others are converted. Christ came that we may have life and have it in abundance. Our fullness of life comes from His fullness of love.

Christ's desire on the cross was our freedom. And this freedom is attained from His love; not by loving safely, but by taking the risk to love Him and in turn, desiring to be spent on behalf of learning to love others.

MY MORNING BLESSING

GEORGE FOX UNIVERSITY

I excitedly told God when I had finished sorting out my schedule, "See that hour right in the middle of the day Lord, that's all yours." And it actually was…for about a week! But inevitably, the meetings, lectures and various other options gradually started popping up, and the old "quiet time" was pushed off until later. I began using that mid-day hour to catch up on schoolwork, while assuring God that I'd sit down with Him at night, or when stuff became less hectic. Well, of course things never got less hectic, and the nights always seemed to bring more distractions, like late night conversations with the girl down the hall, or late-night video games with the guys on my hall. Point being, my quiet times were constantly put off until the next day and became consistently neglected.

After finally being convicted, or at least finally hearing the conviction, I realized how much I missed my daily times with God and how I really wanted and needed to get back on track. I guess more importantly though, I realized how much God missed this time with me. All my Father wants is for me to realize His presence and remember Him throughout my day. He just wants to talk to His child.

A few of my friends suggested spending time with God right before bed. Unfortunately, I quickly realized that this too, was not going to work for me. Oftentimes the busiest hours of our college schedules are from about ten at night to two in the morning. I was too tired to set my alarm at this hour of the night, much less to read and pray. Plus, even when I did commit to spending that time with the Lord, I found it hard to find any quiet place to get alone with God and when I did, I'd fall asleep. The constant presence of pretty girls, loud hall mates, or even just the lull of a TV in the background, made it next to impossible for me to find a place where silence could be heard. In other words, a place where I could hear the voice of God. Thankfully, a guy discipling me during this time rekindled the idea of me getting up early in the morning to spend time with the Lord? He suggested that I get up before class, to study the word and pray at eight thirty...a.m. that is.

Of course I thought the idea was ridiculous, as just about any normal college student would think. But I was quickly reminded that for one, I wasn't just a "normal college student." I was a follower of Christ and thus lived for a different reason and by different standards. I was also wisely encouraged by an indisputable text—scripture. Psalm 5:3 says, "In the morning, O LORD, you hear my voice; in the morning I lay my requests before you and wait in expectation." Similarly, Mark 1:35 reads, "Very early in the morning, while it was still dark, Jesus got up, left the house and went off to a solitary place, where he prayed."

My decision came down to a simple choice: Which was more important to me, an extra hour of sleep, or spending time communicating with my Creator, and the Creator of the universe? With this perspective, it was obviously not a very hard choice. I trusted that if I made a conscious effort toward giving the Lord one hour of my daily 24 hours, He would no doubt bless my willingness. It didn't take long to realize that this assumption was exactly right. It's honestly been crazy how faithfully God has blessed my times with Him, through joys, convictions, revelations, opportunities and certainly surprises. My times in the morning with God have become not just a need in my life, but an incredible desire. Wherever we are, the Lord is always willing and wanting to meet with us, but it's a matter of when we will be willing and wanting to connect with and enjoy the absolute treasure of meeting Him.

Early in my freshmen year, I asked myself a question and intentionally wrote it down, knowing that I should never forget it: "When will I realize the magnitude of time with God?" The Lord of all creation desperately desires and even longs to have an intimate relationship with you and me. Believe it, or not, that is actually what we were created for. It's easy to relate this situation to our temporal lives. How can we expect to come to know a person if we don't spend time with him or her? And likewise, how can we get to know God if we don't spend time with Him? The Lord has engrained this sweet truth in my heart during college; and I know that the closer I draw to Him, the more I will desire and appreciate the sacred hours, let alone moments, that I am in His presence.

GARY

PENN STATE UNIVERSITY

He was gay. Not a "closet gay" or a "let's build our friendship and I'll tell you this secret later gay," but a proud, outwardly flamboyant, homosexual male. In one of the first conversations I had with this second-year roommate of mine, he adamantly shared with me about his experience and identity as a gay male. Granted, I've always felt that I was a pretty open-minded, relatively liberal and well-traveled Christian. But I must admit, I was quite shocked at God for throwing this one my way. Although I'd certainly heard a lot of opinions on gays and the Church, and actually felt relatively confident of my stance on the issue, I'd never actually talked to a gay, let alone *lived* with one. Even though I can't say this was exactly what I expected for my college dorm experience, there was never a moment when I doubted God's hand leading the situation.

Gary and I got along from the start. I tried to remain open to his lifestyle and likewise, he was always very courteous of mine. We explained our beliefs and values very early on, just to lay everything on the table and not have any mid-year surprises. I must say one of the funniest, or should I say awkward, nights of the year was Valentine's Day. I invited a girl over for dinner and he simultaneously invited a guy over to watch a movie. As it turned out, we all had a really great time together.

Gary actually enjoyed the fact that I was a Christian and even began asking some core questions about the gospel and about the life of Christ. He had been raised in an agnostic home and only had the knowledge of Christians as the "anti-gay" group. The more I hung around with his friends, and similarly the more I talked with my Christian friends, I realized how true this sentiment really was.

It sounds bold and maybe outlandish, but I think Christians can be the most disunified and judgmental people on this planet. These are two facets that grossly oppose the life and teaching of our Savior. Being gay may be difficult to understand or to accept as being wrong. But nonetheless, being gay is a behavior, or a nature, that separates us from God. Thus, being gay is a sin. It is a sin just as my being a jealous and prideful person is a sin. But does my church and body of fellowship turn me away because I am a sinner? No! This is the very reason that I need fellowship and community and the very reason that Christ died in the first place! As he tell us in Luke 5:31, "It is not the healthy who need a doctor, but the sick," and in Romans 3:23, "For all have sinned and fall short of the glory of God." The body of believers acts specifically for support, encouragement, accountability and prayer, further seeking God's freedom over these areas of our lives.

There are a lot of people who struggle with homosexual or bisexual tendencies. By digging more deeply into the roots and difficulties of the gay lifestyle, God even led me to some guys in my ministry who were struggling with this very sin. It's not an easy issue to confront. And it's certainly not one that we as Christians often mention. But as I continue to see the power of prayer and intervention in the lives of these individuals, I become more convinced of God's desire for us to love and pray for them, as creations of His hand. Gary was one of the biggest blessings of my dorm experience. I honestly believe that he will soon become a Christian and continue to seek God's daily deliverance from this grip on his life. We both know that like any stronghold, he has a long journey ahead and one that he may fight for his entire life. But fixing our gaze on the infinite power of the cross will not fail us. What was done at Calvary was neither a simple, nor a bound act, and nothing on earth can stand against it. "Who shall separate us from the love of Christ? Shall trouble or hardship or persecution or famine or nakedness or danger or sword?...No, in all these things we are more than conquerors through him who loved us" (Romans 8:35, 37).

LOSING SIGHT OF GRACE

WASHINGTON UNIVERSITY

I thought I was relatively tolerant of the girls on my hall. I knew they drank, smoked and did things with guys I hadn't even conceived of, but I remained civil to them and just avoided their company as much as possible. They would do their thing on weekend nights and I would do mine. One fall day, however, about half way through the semester, I came to see this avoidance in a painfully new light.

It seemed like a typical Sunday morning, where no one would wake until noon, making my church preparations a somewhat peaceful and certainly quiet experience. That morning, however, I was surprised to hear the hall door open abruptly, followed by the loud and loquacious sound of three girls' voices. They stumbled into the bathroom, carrying a strong odor of alcohol and cigarette smoke, while their poor outfits looked more like sheets of material than actual clothing. Two of the girls headed straight for the toilet. One glanced at me briefly, and all three looked extremely embarrassed to see me. The third girl headed to the farthest sink, avoiding any eye or vocal contact. I finally spoke up and asked if everything was okay, or if my sick hall mates needed anything.

After an empty glare, the girl at the sink calmly responded, "Are you kidding? You're actually interested in how we're doing? You've noticed something other than your church activities or perfect little life? In fact," her voice becoming increasingly cynical and sarcastic, but equally serious, "I can't even believe you're talking to the "bad girls," knowing that you're so good and would never want to be associated with us."

In that moment, it hit me like a ton of bricks just how far I was living from the gospel. My thoughts were immediately taken to numerous stories of Christ. I couldn't help but realize that throughout the Bible, it was actually the most wretched people who were drawn to Him. It was the most cast out that flocked to His feet. And it was these special people that Jesus so passionately loved and served throughout His days. Where had I gone astray? When did I conclude that I was over and above these girls in my dorm? How, as a Christian, had I lost sight of imitating Christ?

I slowly walked out of the bathroom that morning, sad and confused about what had happened. Christ died for the sins of the world—not for we who seem to have it all together, who act as if we're above and beyond the home-less, the prostitutes, the drug addicts and the drunkards. In fact, that morning, I was convinced that Jesus' death on the cross related more to those girls in the bathroom than it ever had to me. "He came that they might have life." And it was my job to abide in Him and allow His ways to flow out in my life. But my life had become so cluttered and blinded by what I was doing to better myself as a Christian, that I completely lost sight of the glorious gospel. I had lost recognition for the immense love and acceptance that these girls inherently desired. I had lost sight of the meaning of grace.

All I could do was return to my room, kneel down on that rutty carpet and pour out my confessions before a loving Father in heaven. My tears came with joy, as I was overcome with new meanings of grace in my life and more so, in the lives of the girls on my hall. Rebuilding charac-ter and trust is something that takes a long of time. I can't say that these girls would immediately and unashamedly run to me now, before anyone else, but I can only hope that

I at least provide that open door where they can find acceptance and love and not accusation and pride. For as Jesus
said, "It is not those who are well who need a physician, but
those who are sick. I have not come to call the righteous but
sinners to repentance" (Luke 5:31-32-New American
Standard Bible).

HIS LOVE FIRST

SOUTHERN METHODIST UNIVERSITY

God allowed me some of the most unbelievable and
life-altering opportunities to witness while living in the
dorms. I definitely saw His miraculous intervention numerous times, but through these opportunities, there was something even more fundamental that God was trying to teach
me—His love for us. I realized that this is the single most
amazing and awe striking part of any Christian's testimony.
The love of God, in fact, is the sheer thesis of a Christian
testimony.

What would your witness be without the love of
God? In college we face temptations like never before. The
opportunities for sin abound. Sometimes they intrude so
vehemently, that nothing in and of our own power could sustain us. Indeed there is nothing to sustain you but the love
of God. That is the hope that is set before us. If you run
toward another end, you will inevitably fall, and without a
foundational knowledge before you, you cannot rise again.
I love how Paul says in Romans, "For I am convinced that
neither death nor life, neither angels nor demons, neither the
present nor the future, nor any powers, neither height nor
depth, nor anything else in all creation, will be able to separate us from the love of God that is in Christ Jesus our Lord"

(Romans 8:38-39).

C. S. Lewis wrote, "I am a safety-first creature. Of all arguments against love, none makes so strong an appeal as 'Careful, you might get hurt'" (*The Four Loves*, page 120). This, in short, sums up my nature and the way I have lived for too long. I've been very independent and have essentially cast out the need to depend on a person. In so doing, I've denied my need for Christ. Basically, I said, "Man shall not hurt me for I shall not allow myself to get hurt." Yet, if we don't accept that need, we will never really experience the love of Christ, and, in turn, if we don't experience the love of Jesus, our hearts will never be broken for the lost.

The heart of Christ is for the lost; He came to seek and to save that which was lost. His heart was broken for them and thus His body was broken for them. At this point in my life, "the lost" are the girls on my hall, let alone those who surround me on campus. I struggled for so long, trying to avoid sin, simply by refusing to open my heart to God and His creation in mankind. But as the Lord began to break me, I was able to surrender my love to Him first and then to others. God offers us so much more than simply the desire, let alone the power not to sin; He offers us the joy of fellowship with Him and the profound ability to love another.

My college experience has been extremely difficult academically. My dorm experience has been even more difficult. Sex and alcohol are the favorite pastimes, and school is rarely a priority. My hall mates' behaviors opened my eyes to the ravishing effects of a sexually transmitted disease, the disgusting mess caused by a night of partying and irresponsible drinking. In short, I came into personal contact with the unlovely as I never had before. It broke my heart and yet so often, the fear of my flesh kept my witness silent. This caused more and more frustration as the semester went on. I felt an increasing distance between God and me. In maintaining silence for what I knew was wrong, I was doing exactly what I had always been so adamantly opposed to. Incredibly tired and frustrated, I could not conjure up enough love for God to transform my actions.

Amidst this incredible disappointment and even confusion, God and His gentle Spirit showed up for me at church one Sunday and reminded me,
"Your worth is not in you academic ability, the 'success' of your witness, nor in how beautiful you are."
"Yes, thank You, God. I know that" I responded naturally.
But then came these words, "Nor is your worth in how much you love me."

"Time-out! That one needs some explanation. How can that be? I've been striving toward loving you more all this time and you're gonna say that's not what it's about?" I responded, somewhat frustrated.
God continued, *"Your worth is in how much I love you."*
I was taken to two unbelievable verses that morning, both speaking the undying love of Jesus Christ. "This is love: not that we loved God, but that he loved us and sent his Son as an atoning sacrifice for our sins" 1 John 4:10 and Romans 9:16, which says, "It does not, therefore, depend on man's desire or effort, but on God's mercy." These were monumental verses in terms of how I had been living my life and how distorted were my perspectives of evangelism and love!

As my perspectives began to transform, and I was able to understand Paul's words in Ephesians, where he prays that the Christians in Ephesus may know the height and depth and length and breadth of the love of Christ that "surpasses knowledge" (paraphrased verses 3:18-19). The Psalmist David said it like this, "I run in the path of your commands, for you have set my heart free" (Psalm 119:32). The love of Christ is not a permissive cop-out, it a transformation. I no longer agonized over my efforts not to sin, but His love was ever before me and my heart was free to run the path of His commands. Likewise, my perspective on evangelism was no longer about reiterating a fear of hell, or forcing someone to believe, but it was because God created us for living and breathing in a relationship with His love. If I, or anyone around me, is not living in this freedom, we are robbed of the fullness of life and more importantly, God is robbed of giving and receiving His due glory in and through creation.

After that morning, God provided so many opportunities for me to tell my hall mates about God's love for them and His careful hand in each of their lives. And it no longer had to be about me avoiding sin, loving people in some fascinating, special way, or even expecting a mass conversion experience on my hall. It was a renewed perspective of me falling in love with God and allowing that love to overflow into my life. Now regardless of the circumstances, reactions, knowledge or capabilities previously attributed to my hands, God does the work and therefore, receives the deserved glory.

CHAPTER 4

PEER PRESSURE

Do not conform any longer to the patterns of this world, but be transformed by the renewing of your mind. Then you will be able test and approve what God's will is—his good, pleasing and perfect will. Romans 12:2

An incredible truth that God has taught me during college is that as much as I want something in my life, He often wants it so much more. Whether it's a job, an opportunity, a relationship, or even a conversation, God knows what we want before we even want it. One of the beauties of prayer is that God delights in responding to our requests, enabling us to grow in our faith when we see His faithfulness. In college though, I often find it hard to discern, let alone stay in line with what I want to do, much less seek what God wants me to do.

A commonly referenced verse is, "Delight yourself in the LORD and He will give you the desires of your heart" (Psalm 37:4). This is an unbelievable verse, but it's a shame that the brunt of it is often left out. Yes, the Lord will give us the desires of our heart, but what is that prefaced by? Delighting ourselves in Him; His ways, His word, His truth, His body of believers. My reading of this verse is too often, "Delight myself in the ways of man, and God will still give me the desires of my heart." Often it's not even an intentional "delighting in man," but my value, significance, purpose and identity too often lie in the face of my peers.

The clichéd version of this sin might be referred to as peer pressure. All of us have no doubt experienced, to some degree, the cycle of peer pressure being nothing but a vicious track that continually picks up speed while going around. Furthermore, it seems the faster it goes; the less we realize its presence. Honestly, I've always disliked the term 'peer pressure,' thinking it was too negative and even connotes weakness of the individual. I'm becoming more and more convinced, however, of its proper wording, seeing the incredible influence people do actually have on us. As Christians, we are chosen to be used by God to reflect the light of Jesus Christ. But if we think about it, how was it that we originally learned (or continue to learn) what this lifestyle looked like? Most likely, we observed it from another person. Maybe it was a parent, pastor, or youth group leader, but quite often, it was a peer. In this way, peer pressure can serve as a positive tool, though unfortunately, its track of influence is more often negative.

Often we can (and do) try endlessly to please our audience. Too often our value is based on various names and faces, rather than the sheer face of Christ. As tempted as I am to believe that the money, the grade, the image, or the guy is going to satisfy me, the fact of the matter is, there is one Satisfier. Obviously the people, things, or actions surrounding us will no doubt shed influence on our lives. The problem is, if these influences are negative, it's like being under water. It becomes overwhelming. Our bodies are consumed by the weight of impact. Our breath becomes short and we literally begin to drown. We feel trapped and helpless. Eventually wanting to let go. In our final attempt, however, we glance up and see the glimmer of an anchor, dangling before our eyes. This is the saving grace of Christ. This is God's anchor calling us out of the drowning waters. God can't steer hopeless, dead weight, however, so we must look up and reach for the anchor. I guarantee His grace is sufficient to pull us out of the depths, regardless of our circumstance. My prayer is that we would be captivated by the pressure of loving Christ alone, realizing that no other path, as enticing as the pressures may be, will fill our void for Christ's love, that which our soul ultimately longs for.

MY TONGUE

EMORY UNIVERSITY

Gossip is an epidemic that unfortunately plagues many of our conversations. It is deceiving and difficult to recognize and certainly hard to confront, especially when we're in the midst of it. One of the many ways I fall prey to peer pressure is in this realm of words. Not to say that I'm necessarily "pressured" by my peers in this arena, but sadly, I find that whether I'm with my Christian or non-Christian friends alike, our conversations often center around making fun of, criticizing, or just plain gossiping about other people. It usually comes down to me being really good at "looking at the speck of sawdust in someone else's eye and paying no attention to the plank in mine" (Matthew 7:3—my paraphrase). Whether it's about someone famous, or perhaps different, or most often critiquing someone we know, I catch myself contributing to these conversations of lies and criticism.

My tendency is to see this as a mere fact of conversational life. But the truth is, my words are an unbelievable witness, the greatest in fact, of Jesus Christ. Frankly, in calling myself a Christian, my words *are* a clear representation of Christ. My honest tendency is to assume that I'm "above the influence of others," seeing peer pressure as a trivial issue, influential for high schoolers, maybe. Oddly enough, however, peer pressure is not an escaped phenomenon in our ever-so-mature college lives. Our malicious words attacked others at our middle school lunch tables, high school sleepovers, and will no doubt continue to be a struggle in future job settings.

Do you ever wonder what Jesus' conversations were about? I'm sure He goofed off and joked around with His close friends, but do you really think they made jokes about outsiders, or Roman leaders, or maybe even Judas, who would so blatantly betray them? I know this is a rhetorical question, but it helps me reevaluate the center of what many of my conversations revolve around.

Thankfully, God knew the struggle this was going to be for us and gave us multiple passages of insight as to how we should control our tongues. James 3:6 compares our tongues to a wild fire in saying, "It corrupts the whole person, sets the whole course of his life on fire." Now if that doesn't perturb you, I don't know what will. Our tongue, that small pink muscle that most college kids only equate to one thing, has the power to set our entire lives off course with God. That's scary!

Though we will never fully purify our tongues while on this earth, we certainly have the ability to respond by seeking God's freedom over this sinful cycle. I believe the most effective way of combating this stronghold lies within the pages of God's word. Our lips have been "burned with His truth." The constant renewal of our hearts, which will be reflected in our minds and thus our speech, becomes essential in pursuing God's holiness. David says in Psalm 103:20, "Praise the LORD, you his angels, you mighty ones who do his bidding, who obey his word." Cleansing our tongues with the Word will not only renew our spirit daily in Christ, but it will also put a stop to the needless words and conversations to which we are contributing. This will ultimately bringing greater glory to our Father in heaven.

THE SECRET

CLEMSON UNIVERSITY

Bulimia was so easy for me to hide. I grew up in a loving, Christian home and had a positive high school experience. I can honestly say that until college crept up, I didn't struggle with my weight or body image. The college transition was a big one though, offering various new freedoms and focuses, including those that are food related. For me, this new freedom was accompanied by fear. The topic of conversation at the end of high school and start of college seemed perpetually focused on the dreaded "freshman 15." Although weight had never been a concern of mine, various factors of a new and uncomfortable environment lead to great fear.

If you've ever lived on a college campus, it's relatively easy to see how uncontrolled eating can lead to weight gain (as uncontrolled anything can have negative consequences). The dining hall often serves as a popular social arena, providing a place of comfort and security no doubt, but also unlimited food. Not to mention the truthful rumors about late night pizza/study sessions, often accompanied by the latest package of homemade brownies. Finally, the effects of an unknown environment, plus constant conversations about weight, food and dieting, brought to the forefront of my life an undeniable obsession.

Though the idea would have seemed absurd in the past, after an unsettling binge one night, I found my feelings of guilt so strong that I went to the bathroom and threw up. Feeling very shameful afterward, I vowed that I would not let this happen again. Two nights later, however, I was up late studying, stressed about a presentation the following day and sought comfort with my food shelf. So there I was, two months into my freshman year, struggling with an issue, which had now become a serious stronghold in my life.

By Thanksgiving break, I was throwing up at least once a day. I knew what I was doing was completely sinful, much less horrible for my body, but the relief of purging had become addicting, and the control factor had blinded my convictions. Essentially, I had replaced seeking God as my comfort in struggles, with seeking food. And by purging afterward, the shame and disgust was somehow rationalized in whatever I had eaten. I remained very involved with our campus ministry and even enjoyed meeting weekly with a small group. At this point my bulimia remained easy to hide, and I was comforted in knowing I wasn't hurting anyone else.

Already tired of second semester classes and ready for summer weather, spring break brought a much-needed trip home. It included my usual visit to the dentist, but this time it didn't turn out to be so usual. After almost seven months of using bulimia as a scapegoat for my struggles, my throat (and as it turned out, my gastro-intestinal track as well) provided an obvious sign to my dentist and then to my parents of my hidden disease.

I immediately began meeting with a Christian counselor, who had actually dealt and successfully recovered from an eating disorder herself. My binging and purging bouts slowly decreased, but the hardest thing was the renewal of my skewed mindset and underlying control issues. Strongholds are basically any form of deceit, whether something or someone, that distracts our living relationship with Christ. Deceit is, no doubt, one of Satan's greatest tools. For me, this deceit was manifested in a stronghold with food. It became my means of maintaining control, causing essentially ever area of my life to be detrimentally affected.

Whether it pertains to a food related stronghold, or anything other, the sole means of killing it is to lay it at the foot of the cross. The practical steps for this might vary depending on the individual. First and foremost, however, is committing it to prayer. And depending on the "strength of its hold," it will oftentimes require the encouragement, accountability and prayer of others. Accountability must come from trustworthy brothers or sisters who are willing to commit you to prayer. This could be a pastor, small group, discipleship leader, or counselor, but point being, corporate recognition and prayer for a stronghold can sometimes be the only means strong enough for the renewal of your mind and security in Christ and thus a new capacity to glorify God.

DUMB DOGS

WHEATON COLLEGE

It's amazing to me how God uses some of the simplest aspects of our lives to teach us some of the most profound things about Him. You might laugh at this, but God used my friend's dog Sparky to teach me something incredible. I ridicule Sparky all the time for his stupidity. I'm embarrassed to say that one of my favorite college pastimes has been playing tricks on Sparky. I pretend to throw something and he always, no matter how many times he's done it, gullibly goes chasing after it. Every time, he leaves me in stitches, laughing hysterically at his look of utter confusion. I have honestly entertained myself for hours watching Sparky play this game, as it never fails to amaze me how oblivious he remains to chasing air.

Now I'm guessing you're wondering where my

great Christian epiphany has been derived through all this. Ephesians 2:1-2 says, "As for you, you were dead in your transgressions and sins, in which you used to live when you followed the ways of this world and of the ruler of the kingdom of the *air,* the spirit who is now at work in those who are disobedient" (italics are mine). How embarrassing! I am just like a dumb dog.

In college, I so often find that I'm chasing after Satan's imaginary "bones" of satisfaction. More simply put, I'm "following the ways of this world." Whether through lust, profanity, lying, or cheating, I am constantly bombarded and find myself chasing these tantalizing bones. The most deceiving thing is that in reality, they are plain, dull tasting bones. They offer a lot less than the pretty package reveals. In college, they're infinite colorful bones of temptation, gratification and seemingly pleasurable affects. It's any dog's dream world! We're talking, sweet, tasty, mouth-watering bones that are advertised as free and without consequence. Who can resist? Well, that's something I've unfortunately had to learn the hard way, through many experiences with these bones. I think the most embarrassing part of chasing after them is the feeling of utter confusion and guilt we experience when that "bone" we're chasing is no where to be found. And what we do find gives us anything but satisfaction.

Semi-smart dogs will eventually realize that it's just air they're chasing and will give up. As God's chosen children, you and I have been given the ability, through Christ, to realize we too, are often just chasing air. We're following people and paths that will ultimately lead us to an empty hole. I often try to imagine what a dog feels like when he finally gives up the chase and recognizes that the person has been tricking him all along? In a similar way, how do we feel when we finally wakeup to the realization that all our bones have been imaginary and false forms of fulfillment?

How joyous God must be, watching His children realize that He is our soul's only satisfaction and that His hand rests eternally open, offering infinite bones of blessing. God's revelation through Sparky has been a simple reminder of how often I simply chase air, instead of running hard after the true bones that can only be found in Him.

THE PRESSURES CAN BE DEFEATED

UNIVERSITY OF WISCONSIN

I'm a pretty impatient person, and when it comes to sugarcoating issues, I'm just not a fan. This can make me a pretty tough discipleship leader, or mentor and similarly, allows my stubbornness and pride to often inhibit my personal growth. When it comes down to it though, all I desire is truth. I see my purpose in life to know and make God known, and I just want to live pursuing that purpose. So for me, I would call "peer pressure," "Satan pressure."

We grow up surrounded by lies. We are currently surrounded by lies. And we will continue to be surrounded by lies. Does that seem fair? Maybe not. But is that truth, given our sinful natures and fallen world? Yes.

So what can we possibly do to combat these lies? First and foremost, discover who you are in Christ. I had an interesting conversation with my mom last summer when I asked her if she loved God. She responded, *yes.* Then I asked her if she was in love with God. She adamantly responded, *no.* There is a sad difference in these responses. My mother does not have an intimate relationship with her eternal Father. I think one of the biggest reasons for this is because she hasn't accepted God's love for her.

Secondly, get to know God. Know Him through

prayer, through His word and by knowing His Son, your Savior. These all take desire and spiritual discipline. But just as getting to know the character of a person takes time and effort, so does getting to know our Heavenly Father.

Finally, make knowing God's truth a passionate prayer and pursuit of your days. There aren't white lies. All lies are deceptive and alluring and flat out wrong. The pressures around us can be pretty convincing, but if we remain solid and constant in our longing for God, He will remain faithful in meeting us where we are.

I'm becoming more and more convinced that the concept of evangelism is far more personal that we're often willing to admit. Until we are filled up with the gospel of love and grace, there is no way we can share it with someone else. 1 John 4:10 says, "This is love, not that we loved God, but that he loved us and sent his Son as an atoning sacrifice for our sins." Evangelism and making God known on our campuses is about us realizing God's initiation of love toward us. In turn, we are able to love Him. Finally, because we are filled by our love for Him, we are able to love others. The pressures and lies of this world are powerful. But the constant truth we must cling to is that God is infinitely more powerful.

GRACE

OREGON STATE UNIVERSITY

We've all been there. You did it and you knew you shouldn't have. Often it's before, or even during, that our knowledge that something is wrong is present. All the same, however, we fall prey to the deception or collapse under the pressure. And it never fails that the next day we feel guilty and ashamed. This pattern of falling happens to everyone, Christians and non-Christians alike. But the fact is, as followers of Christ, we're held accountable to the truth, so the guilt and shame are far worse. A repeating cycle is born and we become drivers on an endless track.

Is this how it should be? Is this how God wants us to live—feeling rejected and hopeless due to our sin? I'm here to argue no, absolutely not. There is one thing that separates Christianity from all other religions. Grace. Not "if you do this, then we'll do that." Or "if you say this, then you'll receive that." Or..., "if you perform this, we'll give you that." No, grace by definition is a free gift. "But when the kindness and love of God our Savior appeared, he saved us, not because of righteous things we had done, but because of his mercy" (Titus 3:4-5). For some reason though, Christians are often the furthest from recognizing and certainly accepting this promise of God. It's difficult to fully comprehend God's grace, but it's God's desire that we do (and we will one day soon)! Guilt and shame are dangerous walls that blind us from the love and acceptance of our Savior. They paralyze our ability to experience freedom, and they destroy our capacity to live under the uncircumstancial and unconditional love of our Heavenly Father.

Unfortunately, college is a time when opportunities and circumstances galore cause us to feel pressured and coerced by peers to do something we normally wouldn't. Often it is something we did in high school and vowed never to do again, or didn't do in high school, which justifies that we might at least try it once. Regardless, the alluring temptations are ever-present in our lives. This isn't a critique on college pressures, or a free pass to sinning, but it is a reminder to Christians that God didn't call us to be sinless. He sent His Son to do that. But He did call us to be honest and forthright in confessing and repenting of our wrongs. For like any gift, grace must be shown an open hand before it can be given. It's difficult to hand someone a gift when his or her fist is closed.

Similarly, it's hard for God to show His mighty grace and mercy if we haven't come to a place of recognizing and admitting to ourselves that we need forgiveness. One of the greatest sins that contribute to this is pride. Often we are so caught up in making our lives look put together, that we rob God of the ability to free us from our sinful natures.

As Christians in college, I think one of the most crucial ways to impact our campuses is to come clean—with ourselves and with God. If we don't confess guilt and shame to our Father, we only detract from His might and ability to do something miraculous in and through our lives. And in this confession, we will be led to our knees in repentance. Repentance brings us back to the cross, the place our soul's long to be in the first place. Here shame, guilt and remorse cease to exist. In their place we will find forgiveness, grace and true freedom.

A NEW PERSPECTIVE

ELON UNIVERSITY

It strikes me as perfectly normal to have your professional future be the center of your college experience. After all, isn't that what everyone else, including the world, desires for you? The time, money and energies are all being directed toward your future. When my parents ask how school is, my response is naturally based upon my academic performance. Now I know this isn't the situation with everyone. Some students and parents have decided that college should be a time of social development and having fun. As long as the weight is being pulled in the classroom, freedom can reign in the social life. One of these two pictures is clearly the depiction of most college experiences—academics or a consuming social life. In fact, even to the point of dividing the entire college population; are you in it for your professional future or just to have fun?

It has to be more than this, doesn't it? What about preparing myself for the future? Is there not more to life than my job and my friends? Pondering this only brought me short of anything close to a decent response. Meanwhile, my life continued with academics as my top priority, trying to climb the ladder of academics, which would eventually transfer me to the ladder of the "real-world" and "life after college." But where would I go from there? All of my pursuits and culturally driven ambitions seemed like an uphill battle with no end in sight. My heart was not content with the shallowness of this growth, nor the future that I was imagining before me.

After giving up on trying to make sense of the collegiate journey, I was confronted by one who had been there long ago and can now sit back and see the effects that this crucial time of life had on his present-day peers. He simply told me that life could basically be spent building up three areas: my profession, my relationships, and my character. Character? What is that? You mean I can really be proactive rather than reactive in this area of my life? He continued, "Character is the foundation of our relationships and happiness is deeply rooted in the health of our relationships." Wow! So my entire life can be more influenced by a diligent pursuit of strong character, than that of pursuing a profession?

I walked away from that conversation determined to reevaluate my college experience. I had been spending my time, money, energy, and life trying to seek a certain letter grade. I was so concerned with the "big decisions" such as what major I should choose, what my schedule needed to entail and how one choice would affect another. In reality, everything in my life would ultimately depend on something seemingly less significant from a worldly perspective. In actuality it was the most significant thing of all. Everything depends on my character. My future will be most greatly impacted by the small building blocks and decisions that I make in regard to this aspect of my life.

My thought here is that college students all over the world are being taught and pressured to focus on their future professionally and relationally, without ever being told that success in these areas of their life is subject to their character. This radically changes the perspective, from tearing down our character in a stage of life when it is accepted to do so, to that of building ourselves from within and growing internally as a person. This is God's plan for His people. Throughout scripture there are plenty of examples of followers like Moses, David, and Paul that lived life like this. They lived a life of bold character. God's character is perfect and His pursuit of our hearts is no doubt incredibly focused on this aspect of our lives. As college students, may we each realize the power and influence of building a solid character, not from the world's perspective, but from God's.

CHAPTER 5

GREEK LIFE

For God is not a God of disorder, but of peace.
1 Corinthians 14:33

It's tempting to think that God has a few more important issues to deal with than deciding whether or not we should *go Greek?* On the contrary, however, I believe that His heartbeat and desire is to be intimately involved with every minute detail of our lives, including this decision. And honestly, I don't think there is anything inherently wrong or sinful about joining a fraternity or sorority. Yet I will say that the motives behind rushing, or becoming active in Greek life will have enormous implications, good or bad, during our college days. Many Christians are clearly called to this mission field and that's amazing. I've witnessed radical transformations through passionate believers pouring love into the hearts of broken souls in their sororities or fraternities. But on the flip side, many *fall into* the Greek scene and end up regretting and/or regressing in everything they've ever known to be moral.

First and foremost, we should be seeking God's direction. Period. Specific to this topic, however, a question that clearly arises after we've decided to go Greek is, "Which chapter appeals to me the most?" I think we need a much different view here. We should ask, "Which chapter appeals to God the most?" And isn't it refreshing to know that God doesn't *need* us to accomplish anything! His powers are clearly sufficient, yet through various relationships and environments, He *chooses* to let us play a role in impacting eternity. That's a good God. So, whether Greek or non-Greek, Kappa or not Kappa, God's pursuit is solely to display glory for His namesake. His choice environment is that which will embody His glory most through us—and as much as we refuse to believe it—this will be the most satisfying and enjoyable environment for us, too. God is in favor of pleasing us! His abounding love can't help but delight in our happiness. And thus our happiness can't help but magnify His love.

Ultimately, if we're alert and seeking God, He will blow us away with opportunities to share Christ, no matter what we do, or where we are. A mission field spans so much farther than the tribes of Africa or the mountains of Tibet. It spans to your campus and mine. It spans to your dorm room and mine. And in light of this chapter, it may span to your fraternity or sorority.

I ended up not joining a sorority. My schedule was already packed and joining a sorority could have only weakened my ability to witness, as it would have spread me too thin. I knew I wanted to give God my all. By serving Him with all my heart, this meant serving those around me with all of my heart. And for me, the best way to serve God and those around me was not in the Greek scene, but I hope that you will continue to seek our Lord's guidance alone, in deciding where your most effective environment rests.

OBEDIENCE UNDER INFLUENCE

GEORGIA TECH

Growing up in a Christian home is a gift that should never be taken for granted. I will always be thankful for this "head start" God gave me. My relationship with Him is so much more intimate and mature than it would have been otherwise. I grew up with a family and a church that encouraged me to spend time with my Creator. With this blessing, however, also comes a lot of naiveté. Even though I went to a large, inner city, public high school, I still didn't realize that sex and drugs would be so "normal" and commonplace in college.

With this in mind, you can understand my shock when arriving at the Miami Radisson Hotel for my first fraternity formal.

"Hi. We're the fraternity from Georgia Tech here to check in."

"What is your name," the desk clerk kindly responded.

"Oh yeah, I'm Chris Styles and this is my date Kelly. My friend Mike will be in my room and Kelly and his date will take another," I confidently explained and then turned to make meaningless, awkward conversation with my date. At the door, some other guys from our fraternity started rolling in.

"What's up guys? How was the trip," I asked, as the alcohol stench of my not-so-well-mannered brothers quickly spread throughout the lobby.

"Good, man, and we're headed out to the pool to kick the keg before cocktail hour. Come on out and join us when you're done here!"

A little embarrassed, I turned back to the hotel clerk as she politely said, "I'm sorry Mr. Stiles, but we don't have a separate room for your date. Your room is showing up clearly, but it's a room for four, not two as you had suggested."

A little taken back by this confusion, I turned to our fraternity's treasurer and explained that I had signed up for a double room. He just laughed and said, "A double room means one bed for you and one for Mike and his date. All of you are in the same room."

"One room for the four of us?" I asked.

That had to be wrong. Was he saying that everyone would stay alone in a room with their dates? Did I miss a Sunday school class where this Bible story was explained?

Our fraternity is definitely a social fraternity, but there is also a fairly strong Christian influence, which is what had attracted me to it four months earlier, during rush. We had about ten guys who were fairly outspoken Christians and I thought, had a strong degree of morality. But I was shocked to find that during this weekend, even they had planned to sleep in the same beds with their girl-friends or dates. Speechless and embarrassed, I quickly grabbed the key from the hotel clerk, picked up my bags, and scurried to find our rooms.

After everyone had settled in, we made our way down to the pool deck blaring with loud music and numer-ous tapped kegs. Regardless of the nice weather and good company, honestly, all I could think about was how awk-ward it was going to be sleeping in the same bed with another girl. Different options were running through my head. Maybe we could do guys in one bed, girls in the other. Or what about just guys on the floor? But how would we all get dressed for the formal? Mike and I in the bathroom? No, but the girls needed the bathroom. I was lost.

All of these thoughts remained prefaced by the same question: How could all of these Christian guys, who I had so much respect for, sleep in the same beds with their dates? It seemed like at least one of them would have opted for dif-ferent rooms. When I asked around at the keg party though, none of the Christian guys had even given a second thought to the option of separate rooms. It just seemed normal, they said, that at a formal, you sleep with your date. Not necessarily have sex with her, but at least sleep in the same bed.

I was honestly ready to cave into the pressure, when out of the blue, one of my brothers yelled,
"Stiles, some bus that says the name of your town is outside."

There was no possible way. My hometown is a relatively small city. I was the only one in my fraternity from Granville, and there were only three of us from Alabama. As I ran through the lobby, I was shocked, though ecstatic, to see what was parked outside.

"Chris Stiles, what are you doing here?"

As I approached the big blue bus, I saw 25 familiar faces from my home church. I felt like a war hero returning to his family and friends. They found my being at the fraternity formal very amusing as they had just come from a beachside retreat. The main retreat speaker led the entire group in praying for the lost people partying at the nearby pool! After explaining the situation to my youth minister, however, he was quick to point out that they had an extra room because someone had dropped out at the last minute. Without a second thought, I claimed that room for Kelly and Mike's date and we would stay in the double room. I must admit that night was by far one of the most wonderful nights of sleep I've ever had—alone and in a bed by myself.

It is so easy to cave into peer pressure in college. "No one will know; everyone is doing it; and God will surely understand, because there are no other options." These are the lies that I was tempted to use that weekend. I am a sinner, saved by grace, but in this situation, I was certainly ready to count out God. Thankfully though, He wasn't ever ready to count me out. God intervened in a miraculous way and gave me a wonderful opportunity to obey Him. My prayer is that, when challenged to live righteously, I'll never count out God again, believing the lies and excuses found in this world. When life seems like it is spinning out of control, faith comes into play and we must remember the one thing that we can control. That is, our obedience to God and our trust that He will provide a means, regardless of our situation.

MY BIG DECISION

VANDERBILT UNIVERSITY

I had never considered myself a sorority girl before leaving for college. In fact, I had planned on going to a university that didn't even have a Greek system. Well, I ended up at a school with a large Greek system and was left utterly confused whether or not to join a sorority. Since coming to school, my faith was growing stronger everyday with powerful Bible studies and I was gaining a sense of identity in this new environment. As rush quickly approached, I finally convinced myself to do all the preliminary sorority preparations and simply wait on God's thunderbolt answer. Well, that thunderbolt never came. In fact, after the last night of rush, all I wanted to do was sit down at my desk and cry. I was torn. I could stay independent and reject everything that sororities seemed to stand for, or I could dive in and use my sisterhood as a connection to more people and witnessing opportunities. I wasn't confident in my sharing capabilities though and honestly, wasn't sure if I was strong enough for that sort of role. I would be surrounded by alcohol, guys and various other things that I knew would sway me toward pleasing others, rather than God. But at the same time, the girls I had met seemed so sweet and surprisingly, so real.

Someone who kept drawing me toward Greek life was a Cathryn, who I met at the beginning of rush. Even though she was a year older and not a Christian, for some reason I felt really comfortable opening up to her. Surprisingly, Cathryn seemed really comfortable with me too and from the start had numerous questions about my relationship with God. The witness I might have in Cathryn's life was my main draw toward going Greek.

Dreams and fears kept me up late those nights as I realized the desperate need for Christians in the Greek system on campus. I felt called to be a light in such a dark place where girls were outwardly suffering in so many arenas of life. I asked God for a clear yes or no, as I knew the decision was too complicated to make on my own. His sending Cathryn to me was definitely one sign that clearly said yes. During rush I had also been blessed with various opportunities to share with girls about the different lifestyle God had brought into my life. They were interested in why I didn't drink, what Bible studies I was involved with, issues with guys and so on. I was happily surprised at how nonjudgmental and truly interested "these girls were in my life." The more I thought and prayed about it, the more clear it became that God wanted me in the Greek system.

In hindsight, it has never been easy for me to answer 'the questions' and explain why I often do things differently. But since joining my sorority, God has revealed so much to my sisters and how He desires to play such an integral role in my life and theirs. I have endless memories from my sorority, from date parties and formals to just hanging out, or even on rare occasions, praying with some of the girls. Cathryn ended up becoming my big sister, which has provided so many amazing opportunities to share and allow her to see God's lavishing love. I've also learned that my job isn't to get my entire sorority to embrace salvation, but rather, to plant strategic seeds that God can water, nourish and finally, watch grow. I've been completely blown away with my growth and opportunities to share and serve in the sorority, and I'm so excited to see the continued work that God will do in each of these girl's lives.

HIS LIGHT THROUGH ME

SOUTHERN METHODIST UNIVERSITY

Rush was hard for me. I was confident of the Lord's plan for me in Greek life, but I certainly wasn't sure how it was to be carried out. There were endless conversations and seemingly trivial questions. I never knew that there could be so many forms of the same question, "What did you do this summer?" God was on my mind through this entire process and all I could think was, "How am I supposed to minister to these guys who seem to have about three concrete things on their agenda: girls, drinking and girls?"

Sad as it may seem, the dying words of my grandfather gave me the most spectacular teaching for this period of my life. "I love you and I'll miss you." These remain some of the most profound words I think I'll ever hear. So simple, but somehow so sweet. So sad, but somehow so incredibly joyous. He knew the urgency of sharing God's love, and all those whom he encountered felt this. He began everything he did or said with the end in mind. My grandfather was a man who lived a life of love.

So when I walked through the different houses during rush week, meeting guys and answering more questions than I could imagine, I tried to keep this idea of love at the forefront of my thoughts. Matthew tells us in verse 5:16 "In the same way, let your light shine before men, that they may see your good deeds and praise your Father in heaven." Although I knew my love would far exceed my good deeds, they would also be a simple and external sharing of my love for Christ. Whether it would be my words of encouragement to stressed or confused guys, my willingness to help a sick brother after a party, my strong patience, or even my willingness to share, it was God that was going to give me an incredible ministry with these guys.

I think the most amazing thing I learned during rush week and have since learned through my fraternity is just how much God can use me, an undeserving, inadequate and sinful creation of His, to bring glory to Himself. God continues to teach me about what true love looks like and how my light can possibly be a reflection of this. He blows my mind daily as I continue to understand how my peers, coworkers, brothers and friends could all be so profoundly affected if I'd simply grasp the captivating and simple truth of His love.

You Must Have the Wrong Guy

University of Arizona

"God, you've got to be joking. This is not a job I'm capable of. I'm gonna be in over my head. I'm not nearly equipped for work like this. I don't have enough knowledge for something like this. Lord it scares me to death that you would put me in a situation like this and obviously you don't know me well enough." Does this sound familiar? Have you ever wondered what God was doing, or why He orchestrated a given situation like He did? Well, this was exactly where I was my junior year of college. My pledge class had elected me to run for Beta, the position of our fraternity president. I knew that the guys in the house respected my faith and I knew I had leading capabilities. I thought, however, that those were well taken care of by serving on our ministry servant leadership team. How in the world was I supposed to lead and preside over an environment more like hell than anything else? God was just about to show me.

One thing led to the next and before I knew it, I was making the acceptance speech in front of the entire chapter. I gradually gained a little excitement about the whole deal, but was still convinced that God had somehow mistaken me with another person. As the year moved forward, however, I began to see His footprints and realized more and more how blessed I was to be a tool within these imprints. He didn't need me to do anything unbelievable, or miraculous. He just needed me to stand obedient to His calling and allow Him to work His wonders through me. Years ago my pastor had said: "Our greatest fear is God's greatest opportunity." But it wasn't until this experience that I caught a glimpse of the true significance of this.

My schedule was full of board meetings, house and inter-fraternity sessions, late nights and endless planning. But I can't even come close to explaining how much I learned throughout the year. From personal and collective principals of ethics, to ways of leadership in life and everyday situations, God was so faithful in allowing me to lean on Him and never feel the burden of serving on my own. There wasn't a day when I felt fully adequate, but I continually renewed and reminded myself that God hadn't asked that of me. He had simply called out my name and allowed me the chance to respond. Not only did I have some incredible opportunities to share my faith with brothers in my house, but was also blessed with some amazing conversations and situations with guys from other houses and even administrators.

More than anything in my past, surrendering my position as president to the Lord's for opportunities where the ripple effects of His glory will never be known. Our house isn't sober now and every guy certainly isn't a believer, but at the same time, there is already so much tangible fruit and I can only be confident in the amazing amount of underground seeds. I know that it's easy to see how one seed produces an apple, but we'll never know how many seeds spring from that apple.

THE CARNIVAL

TEXAS A&M UNIVERSITY

I love my sorority and the opportunities it's lent to me over these past two years, but I can't say I was too thrilled last fall to hear news of our annual carnival being held in the campus church. For one thing, I came from a relatively conservative background where 'non-churchy' events would never be held inside, or in any close proximity, to the local church. This church happened to have a large kitchen and a very spacious sanctuary, which had apparently become equated with a banquet room. Similarly, I knew the girls in my chapter and the crowd that would be drawn and let me just say that the 'holiness barometer' in that church would only register by the sound of ripped clothing. Much to my surprise, however (though I'm certain not His), God had a pretty unique experience planned for that day.

I had refused to be on the planning committee for this function, but was essentially required to attend. When I showed up fashionably late, certainly expecting the worst, I was quite dismayed by what I saw. I envisioned torn down icons and smashed crucifixes scattered on the floor. Though this was far from the case, the lack of respect for the numerous icons and crucifixes remained overwhelming for me. As I entered through the front of the sanctuary, I was smacked in the face with the circus of music, games and two kegs unraveling in this house of God. Tears welled up in my eyes as I struggled to maintain my composure. My stomach churned and I felt nauseated. I mainly struggled with how detestable it was to see all those people making a mockery of such a holy space. The main room was even more difficult for me to witness. We had invited various vendors, musicians, and artists while meanwhile, thousands of students were drunkenly participating in games and guzzling. Horrified, I realized how Jesus must have felt walking into the temple. No wonder he was so angry at the commercialism going on for personal profits, that he literally picked up the tables and threw them.

Finding myself caught in a curious trance, my eyes came to rest on a sculpted carving of Jesus. It hung on the front wall of the sanctuary room. I couldn't help but become utterly convicted as my eyes met the eyes of Jesus on this carving. He peered down through the crowds that afternoon, into the entrance room, through the big wooden front doors and over our entire campus. He gracefully searched each heart, including my own. I wondered what He saw in me? Sure the things going on around me seemed so extravagant and enveloped by sin, but I wondered what carnivals of sin Jesus was seeing in my weary soul. He saw my pride and ongoing desire for profit and gain; my selfishness and hope for a bettering of my name and my glory. I realized that day that everything going on throughout those church walls was easily comparable to what goes on in my heart every day. It was as if God were looking down and saying, "Without Me, your life is one big carnival too, blinding you with the false hopes and desires of this world."

I was humbled and saddened that day, not just by my sorority's carnival, but also by how much I disregard and remain blind to God in my life. College for me is far too often defined by carnivals and situations seeking my gain. My eyes are blind to much of what God has created and con-structed for my blessing. Often my heart is so hard and full of pride that I remain content in the temporary carnivals of satisfaction the world offers. Too often my hope is put in the things of this earth, the things that will fade as soon as I fade. Essentially, my hopes are often centered on anything but the saving and eternal grace of my Father in heaven. I can't say I'll vote for any of our future functions taking place in that church, but I do pray for softened hearts for the girls in my sorority and that my eyes will maintain focused on the One who's satisfaction is fully sustaining and com-plete.

THE GREEK CONFERENCE

UNIVERSITY OF NORTH CAROLINA

I grew up in a church going home, memorized the usual Old Testament stories and even attended a Christian school. The summer before fourth grade, my family moved and church took a backseat. Middle school was a time of lonely confusion and a misplaced identity. I never fit in and was clearly the shyest kid in the school. In terms of God stuff, I honestly just didn't think about it.

Through high school too, my religious affiliation could be described as knowing *of* God, but not *knowing* God in a personal sense. And as if adolescence isn't an emo-tional roller coaster already, family struggles added to my confusion during those years. I bottled-up a lot of loose emotions, assuming that not thinking about them would magically make them disappear.

My senior year came with college applications, acceptance letters and senioritis to its maximum force. Anxious for the escape and freedom of living away from home, I wasn't exactly diligent in my second semester. As with many high schoolers, drinking was something I experimented with and could only imagine the fun nights it would create in college. My expectations for the next four years were nothing short of one big party.

My freshman year of college turned out to be everything I had imagined and more. Parties, girls, beer, and all the freedom I'd ever dreamed of! There wasn't a care in the world. I was making so many of friends and meeting twice as many girls. And I could only gloat in the fact that I went from being the adolescent dork to what seemed like the hottest guy on campus. Smoking pot obviously came with the territory, as did continuous drinking and fun with girls.

I joined a fraternity my second semester, merely for the sake of more parties. Classes got pushed aside and I rationalized my low GPA by saying school was just harder than I expected. The continuous party life carried on for the next two years. My grades improved a bit, and so did my tolerance for alcohol, weed and girls.

Up to that point in my life, I definitely would have told you that I was a Christian. I knew there was a God and even believed that Jesus died on the cross. College just seemed like a time when it was *okay* to put God on the back burner. It was like saying: "God I know you're there, but you know, I'm just having too much fun right now. If I start listening to you, life will be boring, so just give me some time and I'll get back to you. In fact, just gimme two more years of fun and then I'll be a better person."

During my senior year, God's gentle knock started

to get a little louder. It had probably always been loud; I was just too distracted to hear it. I had come to a point where although I was still partying a lot, I realized that the parties weren't quite as much fun anymore. We would get trashed, do stupid things with anything or anyone and then wake up in the afternoon of the next day wondering what had happened.

About this time, one of my fraternity brothers randomly asked if I'd like to be in his Bible study. Because partying had started to wear on me, I decided maybe it would be a good idea. Six of us started meeting on a weekly basis and before long, I found myself looking forward to, and even anxious for, our group study. Not long after, the brother who was leading our Bible study invited me to a nationwide, Christian, Greek Conference in Indiana. I knew I wouldn't fit in and honestly wasn't thrilled about the idea of hanging out with a bunch of *real* (i.e., boring) Christians.

I pictured a long, drawn out weekend where, by the end of it, I would feel more guilty than anything else. The honest truth however, was that deep down, I was just scared. I was scared that God was going to figure me out and expose my sin to all those people. And at the same time, I had this fearful notion that He was going to make me into a *holy person,* and I wouldn't be able to have fun anymore. And apart from these fears, I knew being a Christian would make me lose the "image" I had worked for two years to gain.

With some encouragement, however, I finally decided to go. I was willing to at least give the whole weekend a chance, try to keep an open mind and maybe even learn a few things. The conference started off with a time of worship through music. This was something I had never really done before. I had always sung from a torn, dusty hymnal backed by a struggling choir and an out-of-tune organ. This band was actually good. I will admit, however, I was a little weirded out when people started raising their hands and closing their eyes to sing.

Saturday night we had an eighties dance music party, which was actually pretty cool, except for the fact that I'd never tried to party without a beer or two in me. During the next morning session, I was beginning to realize that something in me was yearning for change, but I wasn't quite ready to verbalize this. During worship, I tried to focus on the words of the songs, as opposed to just singing them. In fact, I even tried closing my eyes. I was shocked at how the speakers that day seemed to be talking directly to me. It was as if God had prompted them to give a message focused on my life alone.

The conference ended with students from different Greek chapters all over the country sharing how God had revealed Himself throughout the weekend. It was during these few minutes that my life changed in a radical way. It hit me like a ton of bricks (tears) that this God figure was a whole lot bigger than just a man who died for me. It seemed that every single student at the conference felt His power and overwhelming presence that weekend. For me, that seemed unbelievable! There wasn't a question in my mind, from that point onward, that I needed to make some major investments in my understandings of God.

Up to that point, college had been a pursuit of gaining value and acceptance through material things, whether it was girls, liquor, or even just a "tough guy image," when in actuality, my identity and value basis was made in the image of God. I realized that there was so much more to me being a Christian than just *knowing* that there was a God (even Satan knew that!), but He actually wanted an intimate relationship with me—a messed up, selfish, confused, prideful, insecure nobody. Yes, and in fact, He created me for that very purpose and sent Christ to die for the sinful condition of all of us, which began with fall of Adam.

After praying through an acceptance prayer with my fraternity brother, he turned in his Bible to 2 Corinthians 5:17 which says, "Therefore, if anyone is in Christ, he is a new creation; the old has gone, the new has come!" I could honestly feel new life being born in me and was no longer scared, but strangely excited. I felt truly alive and free for the first time.

My house brother began discipling me, and I got involved in a church near our campus. I remained full of questions and far from *understanding* God, but I realized that that didn't matter. I accepted that God knew all of me. One of the most important things I've come to realize is that the life I was afraid to give up was not all what I thought it was. And the life that I was scared to have: the boring, rule-driven life is so much more fulfilling and exciting with Christ setting the pace. Our God is full of excitement and spontaneity. In fact, He created the very concept of adventure!

One of the most amazing things to me is that God has the power to completely transform a person in a matter of one weekend, let alone one instant. Not only that, but He will use anything and go to any extreme to claim us back as His prodigal race. My sin and rebellious life as a fraternity guy was just where God had strategically placed me, before He would invade my life forever. It was by the bold conviction of my faithful fraternity brother that I was introduced to a life with Christ. A life of eternity.

Something I am continually humbled by each day is that as much as I still struggle and question where I am, I no longer need the perishing, circumstantial, temporal things of my past. And more so, I no longer want them. I have found and been found by something much greater. I am a forgiven and chosen child of God.

CHAPTER 6

DATING IN COLLEGE

I will instruct you and teach you in the way you should go; I will counsel you and watch over you. Psalm 32:8

The topic of dating could no doubt stand alone as a book, in and of itself. In fact, let me reiterate that this compilation is not to provide answers. If you're looking for Godly advice on the specifics of dating, there are hundreds of them out there, let alone hundreds of people who I'm confident would love to sit down and talk you through these issues. But most importantly, there is the spoken word of God, revealing any and all truth that we ever need. I do hope this chapter will be encouraging and refreshing, in the sense that we can corporately agree upon the fact that guy/girl relationships can be difficult and confusing. But I just ask that you don't let this book serve as your guide. Use God for that.

Dating is obviously a hot topic for college students. In fact, I would guess it's the most talked about issue on any campus, in any ministry or people group in this entire nation. I can't tell you how many conversations I've had about Christian dating, what's right, what's wrong, what's too far, what's not far enough—well, maybe not that, but you get my drift. Honestly, these are tough questions that often have no definitive answer. We know a Christian relationship should look different than another, but what does that resemble in light of dating? And obviously there are basic boundaries and guidelines that need to be set at the start of any relationship, but what about the remaining, "in between stuff?" This book will not (and frankly cannot) address those specifics. But I can guarantee that an honest searching of your heart, paralleled by the Word of God, will.

My dating experience since becoming a Christian, or really otherwise too, has been very limited. Not because I am against dating, or against guys, or anything like that, but simply because God has not brought anyone into my life with whom I felt led to pursue a Godly relationship. I'm speaking here about a serious dating relationship, not about hanging out with guys, or even having strong male friend-ships. Actually, some of my closest friends at school are guys—amazing and Godly guys, at that. In retrospect, the fact that I didn't have a boyfriend in high school, I now con-sider an absolute blessing. For even when I didn't know Him, God completely knew me and was provisionally guarding my heart. As hard as it sometimes is to come around, I've realized there is no reason to fear or believe that I have been rejected, but rather, am being protected. My God is jealous and if I am seeking Him, He will go to all lengths to reject anything, even a dating relationship, if it won't ultimately give Him the glory. Thus, He is precious-ly protecting my steps.

Not having been in a serious relationship has taught me so much, let alone allowed me to realize the amazing blessings of singleness. First, I've learned that I need to have a solid foundation in my relationship and identity in Christ, before I will ever be ready to join with another per-son. Second, I have faith in the precious measures that God is taking to guard me. He is blessing me with this time of singleness to realize and claim my primary identity as His "bride."

I am a "Daughter of Jerusalem who is charged by the does of the field. I will not arouse or awaken love until it so desires" (Song of Solomon 3:5—my paraphrase). From things I naively did in high school, to watching my friends in college, I've seen and learned how easily mistakes can be made in relationships and more so, how costly they become. Therefore, I will take all the needed measures not just to believe in God, but to believe God, for my future. If my God can "move mountains and speak to the sun (Job 9:5, 7)," I refuse to doubt His role in my life. More so, I refuse to doubt the intimate role He desires to play in my life. If that means waiting 40 years to marry (or not marrying at all), I'll do it without a second thought. One of the greatest gifts I hope to give to my husband, if I do marry someday, is a previously guarded heart. Thus, I will gladly "be still before the LORD and wait patiently for him" (Psalm 37:7).

THAT CRAZY CHRISTIAN DATING BOOK

TEXAS A&M UNIVERSITY

I was not exactly happy to see Tom in my math class that first day of fall semester. We'd played intramural soccer together and I knew of him from our campus ministry, but certainly couldn't deal with the pressure of having him in one of my classes. Everyone would say how nice Tom was and what a great person he seemed to be, but these were moot points to me, in light of his appearance. All I could see was how incredibly cute his face was and toned his biceps were. He was tall and blond, model material no doubt, and I couldn't help but blush at the very thought of him. I was obsessed, to say the least, and practically nonfunctional when around him. Therefore, seeing him in my math class was not exactly a good thing. All I could imagine was, day after day of embarrassing and inept moments on my part whenever I saw him.

I managed to avoid his detection that first day of class, but the secret was let out that afternoon at intramural soccer practice. But actually, that conversation, as well as a few that followed, allowed us to at least have some "normal" conversations. Class actually became something I looked forward to as we slowly developed a completely unexpected friendship. I went to a few of his basketball games, which were often followed by an outing for ice cream or coffee.

I spoke about Tom endlessly to my friends, giving them every detail of everything he said or did. Having a guy, a cute guy at that, pursue me, was so exciting! I'd never had a boyfriend before, or even dated. Our time together became exclusive pretty fast and by finals time, our supposed study sessions were nothing more than physical fun and cuddling.

After Christmas break, our physical relationship moved along quite fast. It was at this point when I first questioned what my being a Christian meant in relation to dating Tom. A godly woman friend explained that there are guidelines for a healthy relationship glorifying Christ. I eagerly read a book she gave me. I finished it in about three hours, and wrote it off in about three minutes! I thought Tom's and my relationship reflected what it said, like making the physical, emotional, and spiritual aspects grow slowly, as well as keeping communication lines open and honest. I agreed with the focus of the book, that God needed to remain the center of any dating relationship. But I was turned off by too many seemingly hyper-strict rules, which in my opinion, no dating couple would ever conceive of following (no passionate kissing!). In a lot of ways I desired, and even felt the need, to make up for my "lost time" of not dating in high school. At this point, because I didn't have strong Christian friends, I was constantly comparing myself to non-Christians or our culture's guidelines for dating. I had never wanted to have sex before marriage, but I thought anything apart from that was fine. Besides, Tom and I had met in the context of a Christian group, so I had no doubts that we were practicing a Christian relationship.

Of course it didn't occur to me to pray about our relationship and we certainly never talked about God. I actually wanted to a lot of times, but was afraid that a "deep" conversation might ruin things. I was still so in awe that he would date someone like me. Although Tom's attendance at our campus Christian events seemed to be decreasing, I rationalized that his occasional volunteer projects seemed proof enough of his faith.

Honestly, I didn't realize how sinful our relationship was until after we broke up. The split obviously surprised me, as I really had no idea anything was wrong. After Tom broke up with me, I was more confused than anything. Confused as to what went wrong, what had happened between us, and what it meant now that things were over?

During this time, I was selected to be on our ministries leadership team. This obviously meant spending a lot of time with our staff workers, who embodied a young and enthusiastic married couple. A foreign, yet totally intriguing aspect, which drew me to their relationship, was God's integral role in every aspect of it. I had always called myself a Christian, though it wasn't until now that I realized being a Christian meant having a daily, living relationship with God.

At this point, I realized how I'd separated my dating relationship from my identity as a Christian. I believed in God and talked about being a Christian throughout those months with Tom, but the problem was, it was the same way I would talk about being sociology major, or someone who loves sports. I also realized that the relationship had been sexually sinful, even though we hadn't had sex. Because it was sinful, that meant I was a sinner. I know this sounds obvious, but it was something I had never taken to heart, or truly internalized. I knew that Jesus died for my sins, though really never thought, or admitted, to having a sin big enough for His need to die. But during this time, I saw that to God, sin is sin, no matter what it is, and all He asks is that we repent of it. Romans 3:23 says, "for all have sinned and fall short of the glory of God"…and then the best part…"and are justified freely by His grace through the redemption that came by Christ Jesus."

I realize now that I went through the motions of trying to have a Christian relationship. But I never knew what these motions should be. I never prayed, or sought God's will for the relationship, let alone my life. I would never claim to regret that stage of my life, because I know the experience was God's way of teaching me about my need for a Savior and His unending love and pursuit of me. My relationship with God actually became good, because of a bad relationship with a guy, and for that I couldn't be more thankful! And about that book on Christian dating, well, I don't think it's so crazy anymore. I've even read a few more!

I LEARNED MY LESSON

AMERICAN UNIVERSITY

"Don't date anyone your first semester of college." Numerous people gave me this advice before going off to school. My freshman year began, however, and I think I was the first to be dating someone. I was a strong Christian though and thought my faith was strong enough not to be brought down by any boyfriend. I constantly rationalized that the magnitude of time I spent with my boyfriend was merely due to being in an unknown environment and under new circumstances. Because practically every spare moment of that first semester was spent together, we robbed ourselves of that special first year time span when freshman are meeting new friends and experiencing the joys of life away from home. About halfway through the year, I realized that I'd not only prioritized this new boyfriend far above any of my worldly possessions, but more importantly I'd prioritized him above my heavenly possession, God.

It's very easy to get so smitten in a dating relationship, that only months later will you realize that the "smittenness" you once had for God has quickly fallen by the wayside. Basically, I was trying to defeat Matthew's truth, in verse 6:24, that "no one can serve two masters" (which in this case was God and my boyfriend, but filling in the blank with anyone, or anything can quickly reveal a stronghold). Once I recognized this, my boyfriend and I decided to step back, physically and emotionally, from our relationship and more importantly, spend less time together. And mind you, this was by no means easy.

In retrospect, it would have been much better if, from the start, we'd defined God's relationship in each of our lives and how that would affect our relationship together. We had mistakenly placed the priority of our dating relationship on each other. I don't regret having dated someone my first semester, for the Lord was faithful in showing me great things through this experience. But at the same time, I do regret that my walk with Christ suffered for those few months. From now on, my dating relationships only happen after first, reprioritizing my relationship with Christ. And honestly, that "no dating first semester" advice might not be such a bad idea.

PREPARING FOR MY WIFE

UNIVERSITY OF ARIZONA

I heard a quote about love and how as a husband, "One of the best things you can do for your family is to love your wife." As a college student, you may think I'm jumping ahead a bit in already considering my future family life, but I don't at all. Love is an incredibly profound thing, and I consider it a complete blessing that God is teaching me about it now. How am I suppose to love my wife if I've never learned what love means? How am I suppose to be obedient to God and "love my wife, just as Christ loved the church" (Ephesians 5:25), if I don't know the depth of Christ's love for the church? The Bible gives us many incredible definitions, analogies, pictures, stories and even songs, about how God defines love. It is my longing to understand and grasp as much as I can of these truths.

Imagine your 50th wedding anniversary. Your kids are grown, now having children of their own, and it remains just you and your spouse. Imagine still having zest for each other, still holding hands, giggling and even getting those butterflies over one another's company. Imagine being married to someone you can genuinely trust, someone who helped define the meaning of intimacy for you. Imaging loving someone so long you can paint her smile blindfolded, or recognize from across a dark, crowded room. Imagine loving your wife not only as your wife, but as your Creator's precious daughter, blessed by the beauties of God.

These are emotions that I long to feel, but even more

so, hope that our generation longs to feel. I'm obviously speaking more to men, as I don't know exactly where women stand on these issues, but I would love nothing more than for the men of this generation to rise up and be warriors for our Father and for His glory. That we might truly seek to be men of God, realizing an indescribably grand and sincere love for our wives. For it is only in seeking moral purity now, that we can hope to attain relational intimacy down the road. My prayer is that in these remaining years of college, whether through friendships, or dating relationships, God continues to teach and prepare us for the enormous role of one day serving Him as a husband.

A WISE DECISION AFTER ALL

COLORADO UNIVERSITY

Michelle and I had dated all through high school and were determined to stay together when we went off to college. We'd certainly gone through our periods of bumps and difficult times in our relationship (and expected that many would come), but overall had been incredibly blessed by maintaining a guarded and solid dating relationship centered on Christ. At the time, neither our pastor, nor our parents thought our staying together in college would be a good idea. They responded with the typical answers of, "You're not mature enough. Maybe you need some time apart. Visiting your different campuses will only make you miss opportunities on your own," but in the end they agreed to support our decision if we really felt this was where God was leading us. So after many hours of prayer and counsel, we felt led to stay together in taking this next step.

Being four hours apart was sure to bring us some

challenges, but we knew that in our desire to be obedient and passionate about seeking God's will, His desire would be to bless us. I'm not going to lie to you though; our freshman year was very difficult. Michelle rushed a sorority and I immediately got involved with a campus ministry. Subtle, maybe even unsaid tensions arose as these two tracks of ministry evolved in each of our respective lives. Similarly, because I lived on a hall full of brash, drunken college guys, I can't say Michelle's and my phone conversations occurred in the most peaceful or edifying environment. And as much as I had known this would be the case from the start, her not having a car and me always being forced to make the eight-hour drive to visit crept up as a frustration. When we were together, purity, both emotionally and physically, became more and more difficult, making accountability more and more important. I realize that this is sounding very negative so far, but God's grace was amazing in our relationship and the positive aspects overwhelmed the negatives.

Michelle and I had always attended the same church, so essentially we had watched one another grow up. Being hours away from one another, however, allowed us to see even more growth. One of the most beautiful phone calls I've ever received from Michelle was about some verses she had been studying in Ephesians 1. Being separated from her comfortable realms of church, family and I daresay me, allowed Michelle to discover, for the first time, where her true freedom and identity rested. Similarly, I cherished her Sunday phone calls when we would share about the teachings we'd heard that morning and how God was applying them to our respective lives and campuses. It was hard to be apart, no doubt, but when I reflect back on these thoughts, I know that the separation did nothing but bring us closer to each other and more importantly, to the Lord. I pray that the witness of our relationship during these years was more impactful than we'll ever know.

God created us for relationship; first with Him and then with others. As a result of our natures however, there must be boundaries and wise decision making when relating to one another. Neither Michelle, nor I, agree with the world's definition of "dating," but I can confidently say that through the blessings God allowed in our relationship, our decision to pursue Him together throughout these four years was what He desired for our college experience. I am happy to announce that we will graduate this spring from our respective schools and plan to be married in August.

There are so many theories and ideas about how Christian relationships *could* work. But I think the biggest thing that Michelle and I learned was that God knows exactly how they *should* work and it's a matter of us seeking His will over our will (or the world's) to pursue this truth. God has provided us with His spoken truth, His Holy Spirit and direct fellowship through the death and resurrection of His Son, Jesus Christ. He hasn't left us stranded, or given us the chance to think our lives are mere mystery, but our Father has our relational plans all mapped out. It remains our choice, however, as to whether or not we'll take the steps to trust this map and watch the route unfold.

THE FIRE DRILL

FURMAN UNIVERSITY

Katie and I began dating the spring of my sophomore year. We were introduced through a mutual friend in our campus ministry. Both of us were very grounded in our relationship with God and felt confident about our abilities to glorify Him in a dating relationship. I was a resident assistant (RA) during our junior year and was also selected as the chief RA in our dorm. At our school, this job holds quite a bit of clout and there is inevitably a certain amount of respect and honor allotted to the position. As the year went on, I recognized how true this was, seeing the respectful manner which the residents treated me and similarly, how much honor they seemed to place by my name.

Through this, God blessed me with numerous sharing opportunities and relationships with students on campus and with guys on my hall. Dating relationships are never an easy topic to explain, but I was pretty open with them in sharing about the boundaries and standards in Katie's and my relationship. I could see that they held an incredible amount of respect and possibly admiration for how we interacted, cared for and treated one another. I felt as though God was being glorified in our relationship and purity, and that it was an incredible witnessing tool.

Some nights when we were both up late studying, or had just failed to see the need for a curfew, Katie and I would end up staying in the same room. It was typically mine, because I was often on call in the dorm. She would take the bed and I would take the futon. Given the late hour and her being an early riser, we never thought twice about this setup.

One rainy night however, smack dab in the middle of exam week, the dorm fire alarm went off at three a.m. Our first instinct was to leave the building, knowing that it was probably a false alarm, but that we needed to follow proper procedures. Immediately though, Katie grew this astonished look on her face and said,

"We can't walk out of here together! What are people going to think?" My first instinct was confusion as to why she would ever think this might pose a problem. I mean people knew us and knew how "Christian" we were, especially in the physical boundaries of our relationship.

Quickly I realized, however, that many of the people outside would not know us personally and would only have the chance to assume the worst. Second, how could even those who did know us not suspect something when we walk out of the bedroom together at three a.m. in our pajamas? It was basically like your mom catching you with your hand in the cookie jar and you trying to justify that you're simply cleaning it out.

The only thing people outside knew was that I was supposed to be this model Christian guy who honored God and his girlfriend by not sleeping with her before marriage. They didn't know I slept on the futon. They didn't know we had never even kissed, let alone had sex. But what else could they think? Even if the guys on my hall did overlook it, knowing me better than for something likethat to happen, what about the other 300 residents of the dorm? What about the freshman and sophomore guys in our campus ministry, who merely knew me as the upperclassman who did announcements every Wednesday night? Or what about the other RAs, who had known me for three years as a faithful and trustworthy Christian? How would they view this? Katie and I never intended for anyone to get this impression. Could we ever prove our situation? Probably not. But could we have prevented it? Yes, quite easily.

One thing I realized through this humiliating experience is that a lot of things could be "easier." For example, Katie sleeping in my dorm room sure saved us a lot of time and energy. But is that what we've been called to do? Is that why we call ourselves Christians; to make things easier? No. We have been called to live a radical life—one that is different and unique from this world.

Therefore, it is our job, as ambassadors of God, to

reflect Him in a truthful light. I wanted to write an explana-
tory email to the entire dorm after the experience that night.
But obviously that wasn't very rational or maybe even practical. I never heard anything more about the fire alarm that
night, nor was I asked why Katie and I were sleeping in the
same room. But that doesn't lessen my regrets by any
means. I think our walk as Christians is often based on what
is unsaid, more than what is said. Our lifestyles and boundaries speak so much louder and more clearly than any possible words that leave our mouths. We can never be sure
who's watching, or how someone might perceive an action.
But we can be sure that any action imitating Christ cannot
produce anything but good.

FREED AND FORGIVEN

UNIVERSITY OF NORTH FLORIDA

Based on my life story, I would be about the last person you'd choose to write a contribution on dating for a
Christian book. I professed a faith in Jesus Christ over ten
years ago, but my life has just recently begun to reflect a
mere speck of this light. There's no reason to display all the
horrific details, but let's just say my dating and sexual life
has been far from pure. I began experimenting with sex
when I was 13. I've been to strip joints, experimented with
drugs, bisexuality and even been in an adulterous relationship. Am I proud of any one of these things? Far from it.
But is there anything I can do to change where I've been.
No. The only thing I can do is change where I am going.
But if I don't know where or who I am now, there is no basis
of where to go from here.

It is often thought that the guilt of sin leads

Christians to God. And I may be going out on a limb here, but I don't think God is necessarily interested in the exact listings of our sin. Concerned and abhorrent of it's nature, yes. But interested in the sense of allowing it to control, manipulate and weigh down our lives, no. God's very nature despises the presence of sin. The word tells us that it is His kindness that leads us towards repentance (Romans 2:4). This truth has radically transformed my understanding and acceptance of grace and Christ as my Savior. I no longer live under the bondage and judgment of an angry God. Instead, I live under the forgiving hands of a sovereign God who is wooing me back to His embracing arms. Does this mean I no longer endure consequences? No, for the very justice of our God allows Him to discipline us in such a way that punishes our sin. But He also graces us with the ability to accept the penalty paid on the cross and approach Himself with the freedom and confidence of forgiveness. And this freedom is something that no other religion, god, person, or thing can, or will ever offer me. My freedom is based on the grace of God alone. Nothing else.

As I write this to you as my brothers and sisters in the faith, am I embarrassed about my past? I would honestly answer yes. But I'm not going to let my sexual and dating failures leave me separated from an eternal, loving God who is calling me to come home. God can't help but remain in constant pursuit of our hearts, for it is His very nature to rectify the hearts of His children to their Father. We, on the other hand, often run away from God because of fear and condemnation. Sin shall not be your master, because you are not under law, but under grace (Romans 6:14). My prayer is live my life in light of the promise of God, spoken by Paul in Romans 8:1-2: "Therefore, there is now no condemnation for those who are in Christ Jesus, because through Christ Jesus the law of the Spirit of life set me free from the law of sin and death." *God, free us from the lies that we are eternally bound by our sexual sin and allow us to embrace the power of trusting in the cross and lived freedom-filled, forgiven lives through the grace of your Son, Jesus Christ.*

CHAPTER 7

CLUBS & EXTRACURRICULAR ACTIVITIES

*I thank Christ Jesus our Lord, who has given me
strength, that he considered me faithful,
appointing me to his service. 1 Timothy 1:12*

I am convinced God wants us to have fun getting
involved on our campuses. College offers so much more
than just classes and a degree, and I actually think much of
our growth during these years comes from outside the classroom. At most schools, there's a club or a group for basically any interest or hobby that anyone could ever dream.
And if there's not, then you can usually start one. This list
of clubs at our school is endless! What can be fortunate,
however, is that these lists typically aren't just for secular
groups, but also for Christian groups.

My school has about 5,000 students and over ten
different Christian ministries. And it's certainly not what
one might call a Christian oriented university. On most of
our campuses, let alone most places around this nation, it's
far too easy to exclusively envelop our lives with Christian
people and Christian activities. This is a beautiful thing and
sounds perfect to limit ourselves to these Christian safe
havens, doesn't it? It offers constant ease, encouragement,
accountability and support. Honestly, I would love to just
hang out with my Christian friends. I could live with them,
study with them, eat with them and party with them. But
I'm not convinced that's why God has us at college, or living on the earth, for that matter. Did Jesus teach his apos-

tles to stay with each other and never test their comfort zones, or talk to outsiders? No. In fact His gospel message was the very opposite of this. Although Jesus certainly cherished fellowship and "alone time" with His Father, a good portion of His life and ministry was spent with anyone but His followers. Christ hung with the lowliest of lows: prostitutes, hypocrites, liars and tax collectors to name a few. His parables were often directed at those who fit His image the least, though needed His message the most. Jesus healed the wounded. He loved the unloved and touched the untouchables. Just as a parked car cannot be steered, neither can we hope for a fruitful ministry on our campus if we're sitting idle, or even living in a bubble. The very commissioning of Jesus Christ declared that we "go into all the world and preach the good news to all creation" (Mark 16:15).

God doesn't want us to be Christian hermits. He doesn't want all of our friends to walk, talk and believe exactly as we do. Don't get me wrong, Christian ministries on our campuses are great, but they are definitely just the practice field. They lend us the opportunity of learning how to share our faith, experience community through the body of believers and grow intimately in our personal walks. They are not, however, going to challenge us in the sense that Jesus wants us to be challenged. We also need to get out in the game. We need to spend time and build relationships with non-Christians. And a very practical place to do this is in clubs and organizations, where we will automatically find peers with similar interests. Practice hard and you'll play well. Don't practice and you'll sit the bench. It sounds harsh and certainly difficult, but who ever said the Christian walk was easy? Point made, I think we should get involved with *some* on-campus ministry. This may be a church college ministry, or a campus ministry affiliated with the local church. Regardless, revival in this nation is only going to happen through the fervent prayer and effort of a generation of college students willing to invest and commit to the body of Christ around them.

The ministry I'm involved with has provided so many close friends and has certainly challenged and encouraged my walk during college. In fact, this ministry allowed for an environment where my ears heard the gospel for the first time. For the first semester of my freshman year, it served as my only "link" to God. I felt welcomed to come empty-handed and was encouraged to just listen to the speakers and sing the worship songs—the same as everyone else. It was during these Thursday nights that I slowly began to see what Christianity was all about. I have learned many wonderful things from this ministry and it has contributed a lot to my growth and passion for Christ. In Ecclesiastes 4:9-12, Paul reminds us of the importance in having Christian friends when he says, "Two are better than one, because they have a good return for their work: if one falls down, his friend can help him up. But pity the man who falls and has no one to help him up! Also, if two lie down together, they will keep warm. But how can one keep warm alone? Though one may be overpowered, two can defend themselves. A cord of three strands is not quickly broken."

MY PASTOR'S GOOD ADVICE

UNIVERSITY OF WISCONSIN

The only piece of advice my youth pastor gave me when leaving for college was, "find fellowship, and find it fast." In explaining this, he emphasized the importance of surrounding myself with fellowship, in some form or fashion. He suggested delving into a solid, local church first and then examining my needs for an on-campus ministry.

So I did. From the start, the blessing of my local church family has served as a cornerstone to my college experience. It offers me experience-based wisdom from all walks of life, as well as weekly fellowship apart from my usual crowd at school. After God established that firm foundation, I was ready to look for a place to invest and be invested in on my campus. Knowing that my school offered several Christian ministries, I committed this to prayer and could only trust that God would lead me to a fitting ministry. Not fitting for my wants, per se, but fitting for my needs of growth for His namesake.

Beginning college with this prayerful mindset allowed God to amaze me in the first week. I discovered a fabulous ministry and have been enormously blessed by this fellowship ever since. In fact, I met most of my closest friends through this ministry. The opportunity to consistently hang out with friends for prayer and Bible study has had a pivotal impact on my relationship with God. Our weekly meetings provide me with a tool for on-campus fellowship and accountability, thus allowing for my growth and development as a believer.

My pastor's advice was right. Finding fellowship quickly was important, because I know from experience that it doesn't take long for our plates to become overwhelmingly full with various distractions. No matter where you are, God has a special group chosen for you. What's really encouraging to me is that He already knows where you belong and where you can grow closest to Him. It's just a matter of asking and allowing Him to lead you there. "So I say to you: Ask and it will be given to you; seek and you will find; knock and the door will be opened to you. For everyone who asks receives; he who seeks finds; and to him who knocks, the door will be opened" (Luke 11:9-10).

I LEARNED THE HARD WAY

CORNELL UNIVERSITY

I don't know about you, but when I finally made it to college, I was so excited. I had opportunities galore to tell of God's glory and wonderful love. Everywhere I looked, there were new experiences to share with friends who needed Christ in their lives. I had more heartfelt conversations with non-Christians than ever before. My soul lit up like a bottle rocket, planning and scheming to win my campus for Christ. Because there were so many different options and sources to draw from, I decided to do a little of everything: Bible studies, evangelism campaigns, open forums and I even started a discussion club on comparative religion and philosophy. For one reason or another, none of these attempts were as successful as I wanted them to be. I would become excited that God had started something in a person's life, but then frustrated when nothing would happen.

I quickly became tired and ragged, struggling with sin and depression like never before. I couldn't understand why God was holding back on me like this. Why were my plans to bring glory to God being thwarted? What more did He want from me?

To this day, I tend to struggle with this recurring theme in my life: I want to glorify God and see my friends know Christ. I want to be involved, but why isn't it happening? God, I'm doing all I can and it seems so good. What more do you want from me? Through prayer, time and experience, God continues to remind me of the answer. A Christian life is more about *being*, than *doing*. In light of this, my first year of college made much more sense. God was not idle and my efforts were not in vain. He was not concerned with any trail of accomplishments left behind me, but rather, with the Godly man I was becoming through them. He was less worried about what I did and more so about how I carried it out. God wants me to be who I am. And who I am as a Christian is grounded in my identity in Christ. In living by this truth, my evangelism and heart for this campus have been tremendously more enjoyable and even impactful for myself, as well as those I love.

WE'RE NOT ALONE

CLEMSON

Very often in college, it's easy to wonder whether anyone around us could possibly hold our same beliefs? My school is big, so there are inevitably many students who call themselves Christians, but whether or not they live that way, is a different story. For a long time, whether in my dorm, at a fraternity party, in class, or even in the dining hall, I felt completely alone in my passion for God. Not only did I feel inadequate and incredibly frustrated with the lack of God lovers on my campus, but I felt even lonelier because I wasn't sharing fellowship with a body of believers.

Hebrews 12:1 tells us "therefore, since we are surrounded by such a great cloud of witnesses, let us throw off everything that hinders and the sin that so easily entangles, and let us run with perseverance the race marked out for us." Wow…surrounded by believers. For a while, that sounded like a far cry from anything on my campus. I spent my first year falling and then trying to get back up on my own. I certainly stayed committed to my quiet times and maintained a steady faith, but I think that's the only word for it, steady. There's no doubt in my mind that God can use college, let alone any stage of life, as an upward ramp towards His glory. But for me, the ramp remained level for a long time, simply because I wasn't willing to open my eyes.

After a year of struggling on my own, I saw a flyer for a well-known Christian band playing on campus. Almost feeling sorry for the band, that we had no Christians to go and support them, I marked the show date on my calendar. I didn't even think to buy a ticket, imagining the crowd would only consist of a band member's parent and maybe a campus chaplain. Was I ever wrong! The concert turned out to be amazing, but even more amazing was the size of the audience. I mean we're talking hundreds, maybe a thousand! And I don't mean the stereotypical, "Open your hymnal and say a quiet prayer" students. I'm talking "shout your praises to the Lord and jam like it's heaven." It was a packed house full of passionate Christians! God had completely blown my closed-minded notions, about His presence on our campus, out of the water.

I ended up meeting some great people at the concert and learning about various ministries that I had previously been too lazy and selfish to seek out. In finding a ministry fit for my growth, God has once again shown me the mighty blessing of community and the ability to tangibly see God working in others' lives. I've been reminded how much God can use fellowship and ministries, not only as an outreach tool, but also as powerful means of growth for believers. He will never leave us stranded and will never abandon our growth. In fact, He gave the very life of His son that we might know Him. But at the same time, our hearts must be willing. So learn from me and don't spend a year of your college experience thinking you're the only believer on your campus. Keep your eyes open, for you're probably "surrounded by a great cloud of witnesses" and God will bring them to you, if you ask.

IF THE CHRISTIANS WON'T, WHO WILL?

DUKE UNIVERSITY

I had a rude awakening last semester while working with a volunteer program on campus. It was basically a charter organization created to encourage and allow for people of mental retardation to gain access to part-time jobs. My job, in this particular case, was to venture out into the surrounding areas in order to find organizations and/or companies willing to support this cause. The time commitment for the business owner was one year at 20 hours per week. I was more than excited to help out this organization and anxious to see how supportive the community would be. Unfortunately, my expectations weren't quite right.

The first five businesses I contacted said "no." With every receptionist, my hopes were rekindled, but every human resources representative turned me away quickly. The excuses ranged from already having volunteer support, to not having room in the budget. Basically, people thought the idea was good, but would work far better in any other company. Being completely discouraged after a week of failed attempts, I considered looking into another volunteer organization and just leaving this to a more equipped salesperson. The following Sunday at work, however, I had this powerful epiphany; why not approach the local churches, thinking they would be more than happy to support such a cause. So without further adieu, I headed out Monday morning greatly encouraged and with high expectations.

Church number one: "Our employee hire date has expired." Church number two: "I don't think they would be competent for the work we need done." Church number three: "Our volunteer support is just incredible and such a position just isn't necessary." Church number four: "I don't think that type of person could contribute to our mission statement." Church number five: "I must admit I think God created special job places for those types of people. But I don't think our church is one of them." These disappointing visits were all in one day's travels. I drove home with tears streaming down my face and a complete sense of disgust for what the church has often become in our generation. There are few and far between fellowships that actually welcome people from the outside.

Sadly, I think it's rare to find a church that honestly seeks to bring in those who are rejected. Has the church completely lost sight of its original role? Has it completely destroyed the foundations of Christ and the early church, in order to create businesses and organizations that can be run solely on money and power? Where is grace in all of this? Where is the love that our Savior embodied in seeking those who are not seen, in finding the ones who no one else wants to find? The world starves for grace, and if we can't find it in the church, where else on earth can we hope to?

I still work for this same organization. It's been a great learning experience for me to challenge the processes and missions of many local churches. Actually, we've even had a few churches, as well as businesses, catch the vision for this organization and these people. I think many walls are finally being torn down in this commonly overlooked arena of life. Mentally challenged men and women are often not only very competent in what they do, but can also be so much more passionate and real in living out the gospel of God's love and grace. Their child-like faith could truly move a mountain, much less minister to so many people in a powerful way. I've learned and been challenged so much by these precious creations and certainly by my involvement in this process as a whole.

THE FAILED EVENT

UNIVERSITY OF VERMONT

I have been involved with the same campus ministry since my freshman year. At one point, I thought it would be really cool to try a campus-wide Christian event involving all the ministries. I gathered with a group of friends, and we began praying about this idea. We sent out a lot of emails in an attempt to draw students from the various on-campus Christian groups and organizations. This wasn't highly successful, but we proceeded with our planning meetings and event preparations.

Knowing that our school is quite diverse, we tried to incorporate a unique blend of speakers, musicians and advertising ideas. Overall, I think we did a pretty good job of this, considering the planning team drew from only two ministries. Our global perspectives could only stretch so far, but we did cater to various people groups and styles of worship. A local church donated very professional and eye appealing advertising for the event. Ultimately though, the event could be summed up as a flop. Not that God didn't work wonders in some students' hearts that week; but in terms of sparking a revival on our campus, it didn't quite happen.

I'm a pretty realistic person and I realize that one event is typically not going to be the reviving draw that ignites God's presence on a campus. Without going into details, I can say that this event might have done more harm than good for our campus that year. And it wasn't until many months after the event that I realized this.

We had tried to bring lost students to a place of love and acceptance. But unfortunately the Christian organizations and ministries on our campus were lost from one another. I realized from a personal standpoint that I had no idea what the other ministries do, who they seek, or their vision for our campus. All I cared about was my ministry and it's successes. I didn't know students in the other ministries, and more striking to me, there was a lack of cohesion between the staffs of the various ministries. This was a rude awakening for me. As Christians, aren't we all supposedly working on the same team—serving as God's ambassadors—ministering as His people to reach the given ministry ground on which we've been planted? Don't we all have the same dreams and hopes at the end of the day? And if this is the case, we are clearly held accountable to praying for and at least knowing something about our brothers and sisters in Christ on the same campus.

This is not to say that all campus ministries should meet weekly and try to be one, big, happy family. I don't think any of us is that naïve. But it is to say that we represent the body of Christ and until we can come around and embrace that truth, there can never be an overly powerful event for God on any campus. We are certainly not called to sameness in our Christian lives. But we are called to oneness in a belief and recognition of the name of Jesus Christ. The only way this unity can take hold is if we would start, step by step, to know others on our campuses and to encourage one another in pursuing our goal set forth by Jesus Christ.

MARTHA BROWN

LAFAYETTE COLLEGE

I hate to admit it, but college has a tendency to become one of the most self-focused and self-absorbed periods of one's life. This isn't too hard to understand if you simply think about the nature of a college and it's enormous potential for personal growth and development. And there is a point where we need to focus on personal investments. In fact, the first advice I gave to my freshman small group was to spend that year primarily settling, serving and strengthening their personal walks with the Lord, as opposed to trying to change the campus blind-sighted.

At the same time however, becoming enveloped in a bubble of Christian clones, or even a bubble of selfishness, is far too easy to get trapped in during college. For me, it took two years to realize there might be someone in need outside the limited worldviews of my campus ministry—perhaps maybe even in the room next door. Surprisingly, I was very involved in community outreach and service projects in high school, but somehow college coerced me into an enchantment with my own little world. Basically, I was good at loving those who loved me, but it was my enemies that I didn't know how to love, to do good toward, or to lend to without expecting to get anything back (Luke 6:32, 35—my paraphrase). It wasn't until my social justice professor assigned ten hours of community work that my heart was rekindled for a life of servanthood.

The first day I showed up at her nursing home, Martha Brown was the most hard-hearted, raspy-voiced, Grinch who probably stole the whole year, not just Christmas! When I walked in her room for my first required hour service, she couldn't have said more than two words to me. When she finally made eye contact, it was a look sure to kill! Martha was angry. She was old and seemed ready to die, wanting nothing to do with a pompous college student like myself. In fact, the high point of that afternoon was the hall nurse suggesting that I come during lunch the next week; at least providing me some decent, free food.

I did return the next week, and even decided to bring Martha some non-hospital food. I can't say it did much good, although her noticeably aged lips did manage to choke out the words "thank you." On my third visit, I decided it wouldn't hurt to inquire about the photos on her dresser. Well, as it turned out, it did hurt, but I guess you'd call it a "good hurt." It didn't take much for Martha to open up about many of the difficult family situations she had endured. Her husband of 33 years had died of prostate cancer 15 years back, and for the next 10 years she lived with her eldest son. His joyous face filled three of the mounted frames, though he had died suddenly two years before. Due to financial burdens and inadequate space, Martha was forced into a nursing home and had not seen, nor heard from either of her other two children since her son's funeral.

In the following weeks, Martha slowly, but surely opened up more and more about her life history. She was one of the most brilliant, cultured and well-traveled people I had ever met. Not only did this woman have an incredible faith and personal testimony, but her path had also encountered war, sickness, pain and tragedy—all forms of suffering that I had rarely come into contact with. Each successive week that I visited Martha, it was as if layers of her hardened shell were peeled back. By the tenth week, after two hours of laughing and crying, I knew that it wouldn't be the last I saw of Martha Brown.

I will graduate this year and can guarantee that Martha will be present at my graduation commencement. It may take a procession of nurses to get her where she needs to be, but I wouldn't be surprised to see her wheelchair in the front row. This woman has not only been the most influential mentor in my life, but she has also been an amazing confidant and friend. I'm sure I would have done fine living in my little enclave of Christian college students throughout my four years. But the opportunity to branch out and allow God to use a woman who was a little older and a little wiser has been irreplaceable. Martha Brown allowed my college experience to be enriched with wisdom and perspective that I otherwise would never have encountered. Fortunately I had been forced off my comfortable, self-centered pedestal, which was inhibiting my life and my faith from spreading its wings and flying.

In retrospect, I realize that this flying could have taken the route of various other organizations or volunteer groups. It could have included starving children, tired housewives, jobless, homeless, helpless, or hopeless anybodies. My mover wasn't Martha, although God did use her in an incredible way to challenge and change my heart. My mover was actually my very Maker. God knew I needed a changed perspective. My gaze needed to move from myself to the humble, servitude of my Savior, which would result in a gaze towards the other. It wasn't Martha Brown's heart that was necessarily hardened, but it was my heart. Although it's a lesson that often must be experienced firsthand, my prayer is that your heart and mine would never become hardened to the constant needs of those around us. For the fact of the matter is: Everyone wants to be loved. And God's love is abundantly capable, but we need the willing desire to embrace His love and in return, be able to extend it.

CHAPTER 8

COLLEGE SPORTS

*Similarly, if anyone competes as an athlete, he does not
receive the victor's crown unless he competes
according to the rules (2 Timothy 2:5).*

Playing college sports can be an incredible experience. Obviously it's a lot of work, but work which hopefully brings enjoyment and success, both physically and emotionally. With that success, however, come a lot of other
things. In playing college tennis, I would often need to ask
myself why I was playing, and more importantly, for
whom? Was it for the love of the game, the competition, or
attention and recognition? But most of all, was it for God?

Literally stepping back from the playing field and
looking at the big picture often sheds light on the unnotice-
able things. For example, were the numerous hours spent
with my team, practicing, traveling, competing and socializ-
ing used to exhibit and share the love of Christ, or something else?

There is certainly a needed balance between constantly preaching to our friends, versus being a "normal"
team player and college student, who allows God to initiate
conversations and sharing opportunities. In my opinion,
one of the biggest misconceptions of evangelism, on the
sports field or elsewhere, is that it's an acquired skill or
behavior of some sort. I think the heart of evangelism is
falling in love and thus alignment with the heart of God. It
is knowing this love that floods and compels it to spill into
everyday relationships and interactions.

This issue isn't at all specific to a tennis team, or a

given college. As Christians, we are constantly searching for the right balance between what is relational evangelism that truly reflects Christ, and what is preachy, street corner evangelism, which tends to turn people away. Maybe I will never see every girl on my tennis team become a Christian, but in consciously asking for a renewed identity of who I am in Christ, my focus is shifted toward being a light for God's purposes through Christ in me. I can only hope that this grounded identity and purpose will serve as my confirmation of why and for whom I am playing.

My Attitude

Washington and Lee University

Attitude is such a crucial facet of playing college sports as a Christian. It wasn't until my second year playing college sports that I realized how much my attitude could do, in terms of how people viewed me. We can all probably admit that competition often brings out the worst in us. I guess it's just that human instinct that seems to come out the strongest when we're put in a competitive situation. Paul tells us in Philippians 2:5 that "Your attitude should be like that of Christ Jesus." When first reading this, I actually thought it sounded simple. "Sure," I thought, "I'll just be positive and optimistic and surely that will suffice for my attitude resembling Jesus, right?" Well, right, until your opponent intentionally pushes you out of bounds, or the referee makes a horrible call causing you to lose the match. It's during these times that our attitudes often gets to the best of us and we tend to lose our temper, as well as our Christ-like demeanor.

Taking on the attitude of Jesus in all our endeavors

means maintaining it on a good day, a bad day, after a game won, or a game lost. It means that no matter how bad the situation seems, as David writes in Psalm 118:24, "This is the day which the Lord has made; let us rejoice and be glad in it." After all, it is *just* a game and you never know how God might use the witness of your attitude, which reflects your walk with Christ, to impact coaches, referees, teammates and certainly spectators.

MY FALSE IDOL

GEORGIA TECH

The moment I arrived on campus, my first thought was, "These are my stomping grounds for the next four years; where my dreams will be realized and my stepping stone toward life as a professional tennis player will take hold." I honestly believed that I was destined to become the next Michael Chang, the foreign superstar who would surpass Andre Agassi and Pete Sampras as the next American tennis champion.

I spent most of my adolescent years in Taipei, Taiwan and had a very successful junior tennis career. The on-court attention I received basically gave me my worth in life. I loved it and everything about my identity became based on my accomplishments on the tennis court.

Though I never felt pressure from my parents to "make it" as a tennis player, the underlying expectations around me eventually got to my head. I began to feel that if I didn't achieve what was expected of me, I would be viewed as a failure. This vicious cycle of putting pressure on myself in order to please others continued throughout high school and was unconsciously dragged into my first few years of col-

lege. I attended college on the mere principle of a scholarship to play tennis. There was no doubt in my mind that a
professional tennis career was where I was headed, but I figured this last bit of preparation would be helpful.

My first year was fairly normal, though I didn't get
the playing time I had expected. I brushed it off as mere
growing pains and the need to acclimate to the college style.
I assumed by the next year I was assured a spot in the starting lineup and my successes would run from there. Little
did I know that my plans weren't exactly the same as God's.

I became a Christian during the end of my freshman
year. Even then, when my understanding of Christianity
was very basic, I recognized the spiritual void inside of me.
I understood that when I became a Christian, I was to yield
my life to Christ's control. Jesus was to be on the throne of
my life, not me. Yet, if you had known me during this time,
you would have known right away that I was ultimate king
of my life. I was willing to surrender most aspects of my
life to Jesus, but I wasn't going to give up my desires (selfish and prideful) for tennis. In retrospect, during this time,
tennis remained the ultimate god in my life. When it came
down to it, I worshipped tennis, not Jesus.

My sophomore year took a turn for the worst. After
a successful fall season, I injured my right foot and was
forced to redshirt the season. By the time fall rolled around,
however, I was back and playing some of the best tennis of
my life. I was on top of the world and was constantly praising the Lord. After Christmas break though, things took
another turn for the worst. I started off the spring season
playing poorly and as my confidence dwindled, so did my
faith in God. I thought He was abandoning me, when in
reality He was just trying to get my focus back on Him.
Unlike the fall, when it seemed I was able to praise God for
everything, I would no longer turn to Him for help or guid-

ance, regardless of the situation. I became so miserable that I decided to transfer.

From the start, I loved my new school! I loved the city, the campus, the team and all the people. My dreams of professional tennis were rekindled, and it seemed the perfect place for them to begin! But then a funny thing happened. Five days into practice, I was hit with the overwhelming feeling that it wasn't the place for me. I had an uncanny feeling that my heart remained at Georgia Tech. So believe it or not, I transferred back to Tech. As absurd as it sounds now, I've never had a greater peace about any decision in my life. For once, I felt God was speaking directly to me, and more importantly, that I was listening.

As I finished up that final semester as a transfer student, I decided to get involved with a Christian fellowship. No longer committed to the tennis team, I was able to focus my life more clearly on God. I was blessed with many wonderful friends who showed me what it meant to live for the Lord, dying daily to myself and taking up my cross. For the first time, I began walking in faith. What God has shown me since has surpassed any and all expectations!

Upon returning to Tech, I was fully aware that though I'd transferred for purely selfish reasons, God had used that 800-mile difference to show me the unselfishness I needed to draw from Him. I no longer felt the need to live up to any expectations on the tennis court. In fact, I no longer had the adamant desire to be a famous tennis star. I realized that though God had blessed me with talent and opportunity to play tennis, it was in His hands as to where it would take me.

During these college years, I've learned that my selfish ambitions and dreams of fame and wealth are rubbish, compared to God's sending His only son to die on a cross for my sins. As the apostle Paul said, "But whatever was to my profit I now consider loss for the sake of Christ. What is more, I consider everything a loss compared to the surpassing greatness of knowing Jesus Christ my Lord, for whose sake I have lost all things" (Philippians 3:7-8). Though tennis will always remain a special part of my life, it no longer remains a stronghold. Christ has captured this place in my heart and I hope He remains the only stronghold I strive for.

A PATH OF PERSEVERANCE

SAMFORD COLLEGE

New experiences definitely yield growth in an individual. As a collegiate athlete, I've encountered a lot of exciting and memorable times, but I've also had to deal with a lot of unexpected challenges. I am a distance runner and have enjoyed running for my entire life. In high school, my coaches and parents warned me that playing college sports could be like having a job. How awesome, I thought! I would get money for doing what I loved! So by the end of my senior year, I made the decision to run at Samford University. To my surprise, I quickly learned that a job could be a lot harder than I expected.

I arrived at pre-season in the best shape of my life, obviously expectant of a promising fall. Things went well for a couple of months, but then I started having problems. Anemia, injuries, fatigue, you name it, I had it. After an entire year of recurring injuries and failed recoveries, I began to question my running career. I knew that God was in control, but it was still hard to understand why He was allowing this to happen? I was supposed to be running, right?

James 1:2-4 became my sustaining grace during these times. It reads, "Consider it pure joy, my brothers, whenever you face trials of many kinds, because you know that the testing of your faith develops perseverance. Perseverance must finish its work so that you may be mature and complete, not lacking anything." How promising that is! I needed to have joy and not focus on the negative aspects of my life. When I began listening to the Holy Spirit, God was faithful to His promises, teaching me and maturing my walk. It is absolutely amazing what's in store for us, if only we're willing to take our hands off the wheel and let God do His job.

As the Bible says, "So then, just as you received Christ Jesus as Lord, continue to live in him, rooted and built up in him, strengthened in the faith as you were taught, and overflowing with thankfulness" (Colossians 2:6-7). I realized that during this time I had not been thankful for what God had given me. Paul goes on to say, "Since, then, you have been raised with Christ, set your hearts on things above, where Christ is seated at the right hand of God. Set your minds on things above, not on earthly things" (3:1-2). God really hit me head-on with this verse. Unfortunately, I had been so caught up in my frustrations with injuries and pride, that I'd lost focus of my desires to glorify Him.

My second season started off great, but not far into the cross-country season, the fatigue and signs of injury arose once again. I came to lose my love for competition and the job that I had once thought so great, had quickly become a dreaded chore. The one thing I could claim as truth was that God had a specific plan for me. Daily, I would kneel before Him and question my role as a runner and more specifically, as a runner at Samford. I finished up that season, but also became more dedicated to my prayer

life and more alert to God's open doors. In October, I felt
God leading me not to run after that year. This was a huge
step in my life. Since sixth grade, my afternoons, weekends
and friendships had revolved around running. I would've
never dreamed this to be the will for my life, but I trusted
that if the Creator of the universe was suggesting it, I would
be smart to listen.

Since choosing not to run anymore, I have been reas-
sured of God's perfect knowledge of a situation, even when
I'm completely confused. God loves us so much and like
any parent, wants the best for His children. He longs for our
daily friendship and intimacy. College has been an incredible growth spurt for me and though the plans were certainly
nothing I would have ever expected, that's God, and that's
why I love Him. Collegiate running was, no doubt, a true
learning experience. Certainly different than what I thought
it would be, but nothing I would ever take back. I'm incredibly thankful for the friends, memories, lessons, and trials
I've encountered during these years. No matter what happens, I am faithfully trusting God. In seeking His will, I
know that His plans will not just be done, but they will be
done perfectly.

No Longer a Crutch

University of Illinois

To this day, I would argue that football can be one of
most wonderful parts of life. To say that football is a wonderful life, however, is faulty. Yet this was my understanding while growing up and playing football through my first
two years of college. I literally ate, slept and breathed football. From junior leagues, to middle school prep-teams, on
to a state championship high school program and finally, to

starting at a Big Ten school of my dreams: Football was my identity. It's where my confidence, hope and aspirations had been set for as long as I could remember. Being a football player was how people recognized me and how I had come to recognize myself. There is truth in gaining confidence and building an identity from a sport or given activity, but when our lives become based upon a temporary gain, we are setting ourselves up for an inevitable fall.

God had never been a big part of my life. My parents went to church, but never forced my brother and me to accompany them. I guess growing up in America, it's pretty hard not to be influenced by our sub-culture of Christianity, but that's not to say it always has a positive influence. My understanding of God was very "crutch" based. It had been pretty much engrained in me (through movies, media and society) to put "God" in the subject space when I needed help with something such as an exam, a girlfriend, or even a big tackle during a football game. In the most basic sense, I was "using" God. Not that He was ever fooled by my creative schemes, or got frustrated when I "got another one past Him," but I know He was certainly listening. Most of the time, it was my pride, gain, or recognition that I sought through His intervention. But all the same, He patiently endured my superficial and hardhearted schemes.

In my junior year, the football season was cruising along great. Playing as a captain, I was the high tackler by mid-season. My streak didn't last for long though, when any player's nightmare became a reality one doomed Friday night. It was the fourth quarter during a home game against our biggest rival. I went in head first for a big tackle and before I knew it, woke up in the emergency room. The unconsciousness was the least of my concerns, however. I had torn my anterior cruciate ligament and medial collateral ligament, plus shattered a bone in my right ankle. I was out for a minimum of ten months and required three surgeries. I had already redshirted during my freshman year, so the reality hit me that my scholarship would be lost, and my football career had come to an abrupt end. At that point in my life, that meant my life had come to an end.

The next year of life I spent in and out of hospitals and rehab centers, trying desperately to regain my leg strength. This included a lot of time in our team workout and locker room. I had always been so set on my goals, successes and desires, that I hadn't made the time to befriend more than a select group of guys on the team. But it was during these months that I came to know the men I can honestly claim today as having had the greatest impact on my life. Sensing some of my usual post-workout frustrations, one day they invited me to an on-campus ministry for athletes.

The speaker that night had been a professional ball player who had retired after being diagnosed with a severe form of lupus. I think the most impressive words of his testimony that evening were, "If God hadn't been my foundation through both the disease and through losing my ability to play football, I would be dying right now." He wasn't talking about dying in the sense that we know it, for lupus is a deathly, lifelong disease that has yet to be cured. In the basic understanding of the word, this man *was* dying. Yet his belief in Jesus Christ and what He did on the cross had given him life.

He had been freed from the penalty of death and handed the gift of eternal life. Similarly, although football had been an incredible facet of his life, he had something infinitely greater and more lasting with his faith in God's free gift of grace and salvation.

That night was a turning point for me in a lot of ways. I am a second semester senior now, playing some intramural football, but continue to be in the weight room a lot, trying to get my leg back to where it used to be. My life has changed though. I'm still madly in love with the game of football, but I'm even more madly in love with my Savior, the One who enables me to play football. Obviously I still struggle with many things and certainly find myself coveting false idols such as grades, girls, or most often, myself. I continue to be taught and encouraged by the guys on my team who have taken me under their spiritual wings, and I'm seeing more and more each day that nothing in our lives is an accident. Not football injuries, or bad workouts, which leave us feeling down—nothing is a random event. For some reason, God desires to use these circumstances and our lives to glorify Himself.

I MESSED UP, BUT GOD MADE UP

UNIVERSITY OF NORTH CAROLINA

I came to college not only set on maintaining a solid relationship with Christ, but also on making an eternal impact on others' relationships with Christ. And I must admit, when fall break came around freshman year, I was psyched to share with my friends and family at home what God had been up to in and through me during those months.

When I returned to school after break, I had let my guard down a bit too much. Soccer conditioning was in full force and final cuts were to be made by late October. I had come out of high school as a four-year all-state player and had great expectation of starting that spring season. I hate the phrase "peer pressure" and would never admit to succumbing to it, but during those months, I will say it was a powerful part of my life. The upperclassmen would taunt us and treat us like slaves (somewhat normal).

The worst of this treatment came during the "team bonding sessions," which took place off the field. Sadly, I can't even say we were forced to do anything, but I definitely would have felt out of place and embarrassed if I hadn't participated in these "activities of initiation." During those weeks, I did stuff with girls, beer, property and probably many other things I don't even realize, that I think I'll regret until the day I die. But I reiterate, I had *chosen* to do these things. Peer pressure, fear and pride slowly molded my beliefs and identity into various lies and deceptions.

I did make the soccer team that fall and I display in the starting line-up that spring. But as a third year player now looking back, I shamefully admit that the repercussions of those few weeks still haunt me, both personally and relationally. Thankfully, I am under the grace of a perfect, loving and merciful Father, so that I know where I will be when I die and why I have been forgiven. And no doubt, God has used this portion of my testimony in a powerful way, especially for the incoming freshman who are experiencing that stage of vulnerability and desire for acceptance.

Our God is unbelievably merciful and forever just. Although I am not mastered by this world, nor burdened by the wages of sin, I still have to arm myself daily for the arrows that will inevitably come my way. In doing this, I am not claiming to be some God super-hero, or phenomenal witness on my soccer team, but I am surrendering myself to a recognition of my need for the daily pursuit of Jesus Christ in my life.

A MISALIGNED IDENTITY

JACKSONVILLE UNIVERSITY

I was a good athlete in high school. In fact, I think most of my classmates would say athletics defined me. I don't mean that in a necessarily arrogant way, but I was a successful athlete. When I arrived at college, playing *just* an intramural or club sport seemed greatly humiliating. My pride and value system were utterly misaligned, which in turn affected how I viewed my purpose and role as an athlete in college.

My issues toward playing a club sport were much like how I viewed God and my life as a Christian. I often saw myself as too good for certain people. I was too good for putting up with this or that crowd. Often, even too good for hanging out with certain Christians. They didn't know me and they certainly didn't know who *I* was in high school, thus how could I value them, and more so, how could they value me?

Sports had been too instrumental in my life to avoid them altogether, so when flag football registration rolled around, I decided to stoop down and sign up. As He always seems to do, God has taught me an incredible amount through my club sports participation. I can't say it's been about the sports themselves. I certainly haven't experienced the exposure I received in high school, or the state championship ring that came with an undefeated season. But I have come to learn that all of the above characteristics are far from the underlying satisfier.

We are created and wired to be valued and accepted. This isn't a pride issue, but an aspect of how God created us.

The problem is, far too often we seek this value and acceptance in a person, an event or a thing. For me, my value stemmed from my athletic achievements.

Essentially, through high school and obviously into my early days of college, my identity was based on day-to-day, earthly achievements. This inarguably left me unfulfilled. God used my participation in club sports to realign my perspectives. He reminded me that my identity is to be solely based on the vertical achievement won through the cross of Jesus Christ. So whether I'm playing in a professional tournament, or just a pick-up game on the front lawn, my achievements in life no longer define who I am. Instead of constantly seeking approval for being farther forward in a given aspect of my life, I've realized that it's okay to just be farther along. I refuse to dwell on who I was and how I was known, or perceived to be known. But my constant prayer is to be joyous and satisfied where I am now and more importantly, who I am in Christ.

WHAT THE SKY REVEALS AFTER THE STORM

GEORGIA TECH

As Christian athletes, we cannot allow our sport to determine who we are. It must remain simply something we do. This was difficult for me to learn and unfortunately, I had to learn it the hard way.

It was a cloudy October morning in Oxford, Mississippi, on the second day of the Southern Collegiate Soccer League final tournament. We were down one goal to none. I was the goalkeeper and was already frustrated with the score, when hotshot number ten barreled toward me one-on-one. There was nothing in me that was going to let him score. I went down on my side, sliding hard at him like I had

done a hundred times before, but this time the forward didn't make an effort to jump over me. As he picked up his
knee it slammed into my forehead. I didn't really know
what had happened with the ball, I just knew I had been hit
really hard, had a throbbing headache, and was bleeding
profusely from above my left eyebrow.

Amazingly, I was fully conscious; and when I got
off the field and into the ambulance, I assumed they could
stitch me up in time for the next half. Problems started
when I got to the emergency room and the doctor said,
"Here, feel this." He ran my finger across my forehead and
there was a dent about one centimeter deep and the diameter of a ping-pong ball. He explained that my forehead was
fractured and depending on whether it broke one or two layers of bone, there could be neurological damage.

Needless to say I was pretty scared, but God did His
thing and kept me incredibly calm through the entire
process. I'll spare the details of the miracles which followed, but through His amazing love and powerful hand, he
used: hundreds of praying people, one great doctor, 12 tiny
titanium plates, and 34 titanium screws to heal me. Within
six days after surgery I was back in class at Georgia Tech
and en route to normality (some friends may argue what
normal is for me, but that's a separate issue). The pure fact
that I am alive is a testimony in itself, but I would also love
to share God's instruction to me since that October day.

About one year later, I was studying as an exchange
student in Mexico and my friend, Chris, from the club soccer team thought it would be a good witnessing opportunity to practice with the university squad in our city. A bit
hesitant to play again, I agreed to practice, but not to let it
get too serious. I was frustrated because the doctor's orders
were not to play at all, which I translated into playing in a
very reserved manner. The main problem was that I could

n't play goalie without fearing hard contact to my head, which could lead to severe damage. So instead I played any field position available. Before I could earn respect on the soccer field by my abilities as a goalkeeper, but now I had to play positions at which I honestly wasn't too good.

As time passed, I saw Chris's game excel, with guys gravitating toward him and seemingly valuing him more than me, simply because he was a great player. At this point, my jealousy and rage climaxed, because I was consumed with wanting to be the hero that I was accustomed to being, rather than the player that everyone knew. More so, I felt like my reasons for playing soccer in Mexico were based on building friendships and respect on the field, not the bench.

Though my motives didn't seem selfish, they totally hindered my friendships. All the respect and value I associated with soccer had been solely based on my field play. In short, I wanted soccer to define who I was for those guys, instead of showing them that I was a son of God Almighty, and that I happened to enjoy the competition and camaraderie of a sport. There's a major difference there.

Thankfully, Chris held me accountable to what was going on in my heart and my last few months on the team were blessed with amazing friendships, regardless of my positions or successes achieved on the field.

I really believe that realizing the awesomeness of who you are in Christ can help anyone walk more boldly and at the same time, more humbly, therefore revealing that *thing* that makes you different from a non-Christian. It's this very *thing* that eventually draws others to you as well. Although my story obviously falls into a sports context, the fact of the matter is, it can ring true for any situation. Whether it's being involved in a sport, a club, activity, or even a relationship, maintaining and praying for a Godly focus and being mindful of who you are through Him, will make or break your witness in that arena. For me, it is a constant reminder that when I'm on the soccer field, I'm not a soccer player, but a child of God playing soccer.

Oh, and if you are wondering, the guy who kneed me did not score.

CHAPTER 9

STUDYING ABROAD

But you will receive power when the Holy Spirit comes on you; and you will be my witnesses in Jerusalem, and in all Judea and Samaria, and to the ends of the earth.
Acts 1:8

I was sitting in a local coffee shop one morning when a young man in business attire entered in need of his local daily news fix. He laid down his paper in a corner seat, proceeded to the counter and spouted off his order of a medium, non-fat, no-foam, vanilla latté. And make that decaf. The barista kindly gave him his change and began making his drink. As he strolled to his comfortable, plush velvet seat, a dime slipped from his hand. The man glanced at it briefly, made no attempt to pick it up and instead gathered his drink, read for 20 minutes and headed off to work.

Meanwhile, I sat in my comfortable, plush chair, reading my Christian book by a good Christian author, pondering life in middle-class America. What had happened to our society? When did ten cents become worth only a mere glance? When did gratitude, respect, values, and morals take the backseat? I'll never forget a Thanksgiving some years back when the entire evening passed without one mention of being thankful. It was more like a dinner party, than any sort of gathering of gratitude. And unfortunately, I think this is all too often the case in most American homes. America is spoiled. We are like a sponge of resources, holding all the nourishing water to ourselves. I never realized the pervasive influence this mentality had on my life and faith, before studying abroad.

College has granted me some of the most incredible traveling opportunities of my life. I was able to spend a summer in China, a semester in Paris, three weeks in Australia with our tennis team and two mission trips to Slovakia and the Dominican Republic, all in the span of a year and a half! Each of these abroad experiences was entirely different in every plausible aspect. Yet God was entirely faithful and enormous, all the same. His grace and love abounds across every nationality, language, culture and society. My eyes were radically widened not only to His amazing grace, but also to the depths of depravity and desire to be loved, claimed by every person and people group. My falling in love with God in any country different than my own has allowed me to see His passionate love and pursuit of all nations. His love for people different than me. Different than what I knew. And different than I will ever understand. God's love is magnificent. Transcendent. Infinite. His love is amazing.

After studying and traveling abroad, I will never look at America the same way. I will never look at my life in the same light. And most of all, I will never take for granted the freedom and blessing of my faith. Studying abroad is never easy. In fact, it's often an incredibly challenging and lonely time. Colleges offer a wide variety of opportunities and programs for studying abroad. I would encourage everyone to at least pray about the possibility of allowing God to take you up on one of these opportunities. The worst that can happen is you decide not to go. But I can honestly tell you that nothing has impacted my relationship with Christ more than my experiences abroad. Traveling allows us to get out of our comfort zones and out of what we know as life and living. It pushes us out of our comfortable, plush, coffee-shop seats, in order to grow and be challenged in our perspectives, our knowledge and our understanding of our world, our faith and ourselves. Bon voyage!

GOD'S BIGGER THAN HIS WORD

ELON UNIVERSITY

I thought my "quiet time" was the most important part of my day. In fact, sometimes I think I thought my quiet time made me a Christian. And it is true that spending time in the Word, prayer and going to church are incredibly vital to one's growth as a follower of Christ. But it wasn't until I studied abroad in Australia for a semester that I realized how much bigger God is than just His Word.

I didn't necessarily abandon my morning time with the Lord while being overseas, but I definitely altered the *agenda* of it. I think that's a key concept that I should preface this with: My impression of a "quiet time" has always been a structured part of my day. In fact, it very much resembled the rest of my agenda scheduled, packed day. In short, I had subtracted any notion of a spontaneous, natural, Spirit-led appointment with God. My quiet times consisted of my schedule, my plan, my time frame and my lead. Instead of "being still and knowing that He is God," I was "being busy and making God into Who I wanted Him to be."

Without going into every incredible detail, let me just say my first morning in Australia I sat overlooking the vast ocean, sprinkled with diving dolphins and a picturesque sunrise claiming the horizon. Words, thoughts, understanding and I daresay all of time, as I knew it, disappeared in those moments. I had never experienced God in such a culminating, vast and majestic manner until that morning. I had never seen the depths of His eternal and Sovereign power, let alone beauty, before my experience on the beach that day. God overwhelmed me by sweeping away my preconceived, innermost understandings and misconceptions. Needless to say, this was the first of hundreds of countless moments and experiences that I was blessed with during my four months abroad.

In the past I would have been horrified to admit that I only had my "quiet time" maybe five times throughout those months. I'm far from embarrassed, however, because the amount of 'quiet time' that I spent coming to know and fall in love with God, with His creation, with the incredible incapacity our minds provide in fully comprehending His beauty, pales in comparison to any time I could have ever planned with God. Much of my semester was spent silent before the Lord—incapable of expressing anything worthy of His love for me. I had never before experienced this awe of God.

Am I saying church, consistent prayer, or time in the Word is not important? No. Am I saying that a scheduled amount of time to spend with your Father each day is pointless, or even overrated? Absolutely not. But what I am saying is that our notion of a quiet time can often distort the actual intentions and motives behind setting apart that time. A "quiet time" should be enjoyable. Transforming. Exciting. Even surprising! When our time with the Lord becomes burdensome or insignificant in terms of how it affects and leads our day, something has gone radically wrong in our understanding or approach to it. I had seldom been so impacted with my time with the Lord in the morning, that my day reflected that experience. Furthermore, I don't think I had ever stood quietly before the Lord. When I stood before the Lord, it was behind my pulpit. It was with my prayer agenda and my needs. You may disagree, but I think the point of a quiet time is to be still before your Savior and know that He alone is God. This is a hard goal when we do all the talking and forget the importance of quietly listening.

Since returning to America, my time in the Word and with the Lord has become much more real, intimate and crucial to my life. My desire to know and connect with God is on a different level, and I am realizing that my relationships and knowledge of people and friends around me is completely parallel. I can never come to know or love people simply by reading their autobiographies. I may learn a lot about them, or about their lives, but I will never know them. The only way to fully know a person is to interact with him or her on such a level that allows authentic, transparent and personal interaction. In this way, the fullness of the person becomes so much more than words on a page, or a face in the crowd. The words come to life. The face takes on shape and radiance. Likewise, by desiring to know God and the gospel of His Son in a more personal and transparent way, I have to look up from the words on the page. I have to open my eyes to the boundless scopes of God and His ingenious creations of nature, let alone human beings. In this way, my experience abroad allowed me to meet and be uniquely surprised with my Savior in a new way each day.

My prayer is that this will be the case until the day I die and see Him face to face. I want my life to be a day-to-day encounter with God in a new and breathtaking fashion. I don't ever want to confine Him to a scheduled meeting, to words on a page, or to a circumstantial experience. I pray that my life with God will be a moment-by-moment experience of awe and overwhelming joy.

"Give thanks to the Lord of lords: *His love endures*

forever. To him who alone does great wonders, *His love endures forever.* Who by his understanding made the heavens, *His love endures forever.* Who spread out the earth on the waters, *His love endures forever.* Who made the great lights, *His love endures forever.* The sun to govern the day, *His love endures forever.* The moon and stars to rule over the night, *His love endures forever"* (Psalm 136:3-9).

As Saint Thomas said, "The person fulfills his or her nature in the contemplation of God, the whole point of life." My prayer is to live a life of contemplation on the beauty and wonder of God, propelling an awe inspiring, radically transforming and utterly indescribable life for the glory of His name.

WHEN IN ROME

BAYLOR UNIVERSITY

"When you're in Rome, do as the Romans do," right? Well, what happens if you're a Christian? What happens if you don't agree with what the "Romans" are doing? This reflection is based on my abroad experience, but it can be related to just about any situation, experience or even in a broader sense, stage of life. What I'm writing about can obviously be taken to an unfortunate extreme, in the sense that one could be entirely insulting to a culture or people group by strictly abiding to a "law" that he or she has deemed necessary (check out Colossians 2:20-23 for further reading on this). For instance, I am particular about avoiding meat at this stage in my life. But I know that if I ever spend a significant amount of time in Africa, or another place where this food is viewed as a delicacy, I will quickly alter my ways. At the same time, however, conviction is an important and crucial aspect of living as a Christian—set apart in this world.

Much to my dismay, these pipe dreams of conviction didn't match up with the experience I had in Rome. I should have questioned something when the first thing our group wanted to do was get drunk on the flight over. Or maybe when the only questions at orientation revolved around the club and bar scenes throughout the city.

I don't mean to paint an overly critical view of my group, but just that a new environment was all it took to challenge some lifelong convictions and shatter a lot of assumed faiths I had attributed to people. Needless to say, I didn't end up spending too much time with the students in my program. Much of the semester was spent traveling or meandering through Rome processing things in my own heart, or with the few students who did desire to maintain a life of conviction and witness throughout those months.

Most of what I learned was less about the others in my group than it was about myself. My first weekend in Italy was an eye-opener, in terms of me realizing a) the bubble I had lived in up to that point in my life (spiritually, emotionally, ethnocentrically) and b) that my study load abroad was going to be a lot more challenging than I had ever expected. I studied in Italy through a program at my school, which automatically gave me the comfort of knowing at least a few of the students.

I figured this would be an easy way to stay accountable and encourage one another in our faith. In fact, I had even envisioned a weekly prayer meeting as we shared lunch in front of the Arch of Constantine.

Those months in Italy showed me a glimpse of how far my motives and intentions often stray from those of God. My faith had previously been based on my external experiences: what my parents believed, what my pastor preached, or what the culture of Christianity that I had been surrounded with purported throughout my upbringing. As hard as it was for me to realize, I had never come to my own understanding of what a personal relationship with Jesus Christ looked like. I had perfect attendance in Sunday school and my devotions had been relatively consistent since I could remember.

But as I saw for the first time, those acts of ritual and tradition mean absolutely nothing apart from an intimate, growing relationship with God. I think one of the most impressive moments of my time in Rome was spent sitting in a garden in the outskirts of Vatican City. The radiant colors of spring and the beauty of the budding flowers are beyond articulation.

As I sat staring at one of the delicate flowers, I had a profound realization about my faith. If a flower is rooted well, it will continue growing to its fullness. In other words, if it's fully grounded and taken care of, growth is uncircum-stantially natural. In a similar way, if I am grounded in a personal relationship with Christ, I will naturally continue growing and be carried to completion until the day of Christ Jesus (Philippians 1:6). That is a promise of God!

Staring at those flowers, I saw that my faith wasn't grounded in a relationship with Christ. It had been laid in the soil of church, tradition and religion, but this soil will perish. It is a path that will be "trampled on…eaten up… withered from lack of moisture…and choked" (Luke 8:4-7).

I'm not saying that going to church, having strong convictions, or spiritual disciplines is unnecessary by any means; but I am saying that unless the motivations behind them are sought in purity, they will never be fully grounded, nor will they flourish in such a way that convictions become pleasing not only to God, but to your soul. I love how God has continued to bring me back to my days in Rome and teach me lessons about my days there. I hope to never let go of the lesson, regardless of the circumstance or whereabouts. I will do as my God says, not as the Romans do.

A SUMMER TO REMEMBER

UNIVERSITY OF ILLINOIS

The summer after my sophomore year, I decided to study abroad with a psychology program. The trip focused on the study of child development and consisted of three groups of 15 students. One group traveled to Canterbury, England, one to Dundee, Scotland, and my group went to Galway, Ireland, a small city on the west coast. Each group spent their first two weeks doing an intensive study of their cities' respective school systems. Our final three weeks were spent together in London, England, assembling each of the three sites' data and writing a report based on this analysis.

The reason I chose to study abroad during the summer, as opposed to a semester in the school year, was that I truly value my time at school and enjoy the academic environment. More so, God taught me a lot during my freshman year about the significance of sharing my love for Christ on campus. Going away for a full semester seemed like too great of a sacrifice. However, when making this decision, I failed to account for God's ability to work through and bless me, regardless of my situation or circumstances. I have no regrets looking back, but I definitely respect and admire students who take that leap of faith to study abroad for a semester, or even a year. It's hard to have good perspective when you're focused on a four-year time span, but the fact of the matter is, looking at the big picture, a semester, or even a year, is not too much time. The choice of how long to stay must be preceded by a desire. And thankfully, when you're seeking Him, God will give you a clear purpose and picture of His plans. I'm confident that He'll also blow you away with a heartfelt peace regarding your decision, regardless of what you choose.

I think if I had to sum up the greatest thing I learned while abroad, it would be how God loves to work in us when we're willing to live outside our comfort zone. For it is only when our circumstances bring us to a place of realizing our weakness and inadequacy, that we're forced to fall on God's grace.

For me, being in that place was totally foreign (no pun intended), causing me to rely fully on God's strength, but also allowing me to live with other students out of their comfort zones as well. They were experiencing many of the same feelings I was. God overwhelmed me with opportunities to share my faith and beliefs with the students on my trip. There was one girl, in particular, who He gently planted on my path.

Caryn had probably gone to church about two times in her entire life, and each time was an impressively negative experience. She was incredibly intellectual and one of those people who needed to think through and analyze every possible variable and outcome to any given situation. So when I went so far as to mention the word *truth*, when sharing with her my beliefs about the gospel, she couldn't settle for stopping there. Caryn asked endless questions—and we're talking one deep theological question after another. Needless to say, I didn't know most of the answers, though thankfully I did have some books on the trip, which set her on the right track. When she would insistently ask me questions, the only place I could turn was to my own experiences, backed by a minute knowledge of the Bible. Riding the bus to and from school together allowed us quality time to talk and share about one another's lives.

Through these talks, I learned a lot about my own beliefs and was refreshed and reminded of why I believe what I do. Being forced to talk about our faith maneuvers our beliefs to the surface of our conscience, a place where their strength and validity must endure testing. Similarly, it was through these conversations that Christ's love through me could be communicated and poured out into Caryn's heart.

Being the intellectual that she is, Caryn loved to read. After reading through the books I lent her, she wanted to take a look at the Bible. After reading Matthew, Mark, Luke, John and Acts, Caryn went ahead and read through the Epistles. Over a three-week span, she read two Christian books, plus most of the New Testament. This was an incredible witness to me! By the time our study abroad trip was over, she professed to be a Christian. While she would never claim to have a strong faith, I would certainly say that she does. God continues to work in Caryn's heart. The amazing thing is that He was already working in and preparing her heart long before our trip. His ways are endless and He knows no constraints. Be confident and bold and the Lord will respond by moving boldly!

NEEDING GOD

JAMES MADISON UNIVERSITY

As I peered out the window, I could not believe that I was high above the boundless lands of southeastern Africa. I had left America just 24 hours earlier and fear was seeping out of me as the plane began to descend. It was late at night and I was literally embarking upon a new world and a new time in my life. Somehow I managed to exit the airport and find a shuttle service that took me to a random youth hostel in the middle of the city. As I lay down to sleep, my mind couldn't help but race with questions and concerns. How was I going to connect with transportation and people from my school? Who was going to look out for me this month before I began classes? Why did I come here? Though my watch reminded me that it was the middle of the night, my body was incredibly anxious and kept reminding me that I needed to be alert. Fears were screaming inside me, though I was confident that morning somehow always seems to make things brighter.

I knew I would need help the next morning, though my first reaction was to avoid strangers and figure out everything on my own. But then I realized that I was a stranger too, so I might as well squelch my pride and ask for help. Up to this point, if I had ever been asked whether God always took care of me, I would have emphatically exclaimed, "Of course He does!" However, in those moments of fear and pride, if I were to realistically assess my soul's faith on such a claim, it would have hardly been a reality. I had always known the answer in my head, like a young child called upon in Sunday school, but failed to actually *believe* the magnitude of its truth. As the conversations I forced myself into having the next morning became more frequent, daily my faith grew stronger and peace slowly began to settle in my heart.

It seemed like with every new adventure in that unfamiliar part of the world, my need for God become more and more evident. My inner spirit realized that my survival was fully dependent on Him. Accompanied by a hot cup of tea and my Bible, everyday God was faithful in compelling me to rise before the sun and meet His presence, face to face.

God filled the role of providing for my needs by sharing in the joys and struggles I was enduring through those months. Like a love scene from a movie, God and I behaved like a couple falling in love for the first time. We enjoyed intimacy together; long walks on the sandy beaches, quite moments in the glorious mountains, frequent bike rides and even swims in the vast depths of the ocean.

My journey abroad revealed to me, not only the newness of a continent and a culture, but also of my personal relationship with my Creator. It was only in a desperate state of loneliness that I finally came to a clearer understanding of my sheer dependency on the mercies of God. Though I've returned to school and finished another semester here in the States, I hope that the adventures I experienced in Africa will forever push me toward trusting God's promises in any given risk. For whether I know, or understand the destination He has mapped out, my ability to trust beyond an unpredictable outcome, is the point when I believe my faith is most aligned with God's will.

GOD'S SURPRISE IN SPAIN

UNIVERSITY OF VERMONT

Ever since the age of 15, I wanted to spend a semester abroad in Spain. Having studied Spanish since kindergarten, I knew the only way to truly become fluent was to live in a Spanish speaking country and be forced to think and live in the culture. As my departure date drew near, however, I was nervous and could only trust in God's provision and will to use me in this new and unknown territory. As always, God was faithful to my prayer.

While I was standing in the airport, waiting to board

the plane to Madrid, a girl with a University of Vermont shirt approached me. We introduced ourselves and quickly realized that both of us would be studying abroad in the same program. Consequently, we agreed on sharing a cab once in Madrid.

Upon arriving at the hotel, I had a unique opportunity to share my love for God while helping Sharon transport her bags. After an hour long, religiously based conversation, I learned that Sharon was raised in a Jewish household. Similar to many Americans, however, she held some strikingly Christian beliefs on certain spiritual issues. For instance, she believed that Jesus *might have been* Israel's Messiah. When I asked her to explain this further (given her religious affiliation), she didn't know how to respond. She also recognized that we all have a desire for a savior in our lives, but had lacked the courage to ask herself why Christ hadn't fulfilled this role.

As our semester progressed, I began writing out verses for Sharon about biblical prophecies that Jesus had fulfilled (obviously relating to her Judaic background). We continued to talk more in length about our beliefs, and although I could never answer all her questions, I tried to be as sincere as possible in sharing God's unsurpassing love for which He sent His only Son to die for her sins.

One of our last weekends, a group of us went dancing to celebrate our final days in Spain. When we first arrived at the bar, Sharon and I began talking about difficulties she was having with her boyfriend. At this point, I felt God saying to me, "Now is the time, go for it!" So I looked her straight in the eye and said, "Sharon, Jesus is the only thing that can truly satisfy you. Now look, I *know* that you believe Jesus is the Savior. I know it by speaking with you and by your compassionate spirit and love for others. I know you believe, Sharon! Now, what's stopping you from outwardly professing that Jesus is your Savior?"

She looked back at me and said, "Nothing!"

So standing outside the bar, I asked, "Sharon, can we talk to Jesus?" She adamantly answered, "Yes." So with the black of the night covering us and the cool breeze on our backs, we stood there with our hands held and prayed a profession of Sharon's recognition that Jesus was her Lord and Savior. There we stood, chosen children of God, who since the beginning of time had been pursued by the Creator of the universe. What joy it must have given Him to see that finally Sharon recognized this pursuit and asked to join in the union!

Since that amazing night, Sharon's vigor for God has grown immensely. It's not to say that her life is perfect now, for she's definitely had her stumbling blocks, but through them God has remained faithful. I was blessed in being the final piece of the puzzle in God's plan for Sharon's knowledge and acceptance of Him. To this day, it blows me away to see how God will use us, even when on the other side of the world, to display His infinite glory.

PURE

DUKE UNIVERSITY

A lot of ink has been spilled over religion and Christianity. For centuries, theologians and authors have written and debated over issues about God. Volumes upon volumes have been composed, and wars upon wars have been fought, over religious beliefs. Growing up in southern America, I viewed Christianity as a belief system with no consistency and no sense of corporate faith. I saw one church preach one thing, while the same denomination across the street would preach another. For some, Christianity was rituals, for others it was the Bible. For one family it was prayer, for another—service. In short, America often makes Christianity look like a confusing, contradictory, and impossible to understand concept. Because of this, many people stay as far away from the church and Christianity as they possibly can. And I'm embarrassed to say it, but rightly so.

When I went abroad to China, as an exchange student, I still hadn't grasped a clear, unified perspective of God and His church. I was somewhat disillusioned. God, however, was about to change my perspective. I would leave China a radically different person. So there I sat one day in a delicately sculptured teahouse with my Bible and my distorted, watered-down view of God and Christianity. After sharing my faith with some Chinese friends, I sat and listened to precious words flow out of their mouths. The only word that might come close to articulating their understanding and joy of the gospel was a word foreign to my Christian vocabulary: *pure*. Their decision to put their faith and trust in Jesus Christ that afternoon was innocent and unadulterated. They got it! The amazing thing to me is that they got it far more than I did in so many ways.

Their basic comprehension of why they were sinners, who Christ is, why His blood had to be shed and the miracle of grace in being able to accept this death as a payment allowing us eternal life, was enough for them! I assumed they might think it was a neat story, or a compelling concept for Americans. Maybe they would take a step toward reading a Christian book, or downloading a sermon off the Internet. But certainly they wouldn't understand a personal relationship with their heavenly Father and accept it just like that!

My misconstrued notion of the gospel had sadly

been watered-down so many times that the very miracle of its power alone had lost all mightiness. I had lost confidence that, "The word of God is living and active. Sharper than any double-edged sword, it penetrates even to dividing soul and spirit, joints and marrow; it judges the thoughts and attitudes of the heart" (Hebrews 4:12). For my Chinese friends that day, the sheer gospel truth was enough to ignite their hearts for a life seeking after God.

In China, there are no radical splits between denominations. The need for denominations has yet to catch hold. There are no street preachers, no manger scenes diluted with tacky lights. In essence, there are few preconceived notions of Christianity or the life of Christ. For my Chinese friends, their understanding of God was purely based on Scripture and the testimony of my life. The basic tenets of the gospel that America sees on billboards and bumper stickers were compelling enough to radically transform and captivate the lives of these students. For them, the concept of being separated from their Creator, chosen to be died for by a Savior and able to be reconnected with their Father in heaven was the most unbelievable story to ever impress their hearts. For my friends, it was simple. For them, it would be ludicrous to want, need, or stand for anything else, for it could only pale in comparison to the amazing gospel story of Jesus Christ.

I realized a lot that afternoon. For one thing, I realized how inconsistent my faith was. It was like an ocean of waves, empowered by the rushing waters at one point, and crashing to the depths of the sand at another. Instead of allowing the pure gospel to be my sustaining and fulfilling base layer, I had allowed the icings of Bible studies, prayer groups and even church itself, to become my definers of Christianity. The pursuit of God's heart and His great commission is to permeate the world with the gospel of His love. But the rifts between denominations and the battles over doctrines have done nothing but contaminate our nation with distractions and lies about who He is and why His love matters.

My prayer returning to the States has been to grasp a purity of faith and belief, like my Chinese brothers and sisters exemplified to me. I don't want church walls to define my foundations. I don't want cultural, American Christianity to be the cornerstone, or composition of my faith. But I want to see God's face as my friends did that day. I want to see the purity and fullness of His face through the living, breathing word of His Son, Jesus Christ. I want my walk as a Christian to be embodied by desiring nothing of this earth, nothing apart from God. "My flesh and my heart may fail, but God is the strength of my heart and my portion forever" (Psalm 73:26).

CHAPTER 10

RACIAL RELATIONS

Make every effort to keep the unity of the Spirit through the bond of peace. There is one body and one Spirit—just as you were called to one hope when you were called— one Lord, one faith, one baptism; one God and Father of all, who is over all and through all and in all.
Ephesians 4:3-5

Racial tensions remain an enormous problem on campuses all across this nation. From issues in the classroom, dorm, or even among our campus ministries, fear of "the other," segregation and racial hatred consume our surroundings. The easy way out is to deny its existence, or at least belittle it. But the fact of the matter is, that's not a way out. That's a way leading further into the depths of hatred. It's time for a generation to step up and claim unity not as a ministry, or a people group, but as the body of Christ. Our struggle is not against flesh and blood (Ephesians 6:12), and we must radically shift to considering "how we may spur one another on toward love and good deeds" (Hebrews 10:24).

Though Paul was speaking specifically to the Jews and Gentiles throughout these verses, every people group can take something from the following words. If we were to ever take hold of these verses and honestly confess and repent of the prejudices flooding our hearts, this world would be a profoundly different place. "For he himself is our peace, who has made the two one and has destroyed the barrier, the dividing wall of hostility, by abolishing in his flesh the law with its commandments and regulations. His purpose was to create in himself one new man out of the two, thus making peace, and in this one body to reconcile both of them to God through the cross, by which he put to death their hostility. He came and preached peace to those who were far away and peace to those who were near. For through him we both have access to the Father by one Spirit. Consequently, you are no longer foreigners and aliens, but fellow citizens with God's people and members of God's household, built on the foundation of the apostles and prophets, with Christ Jesus himself as the chief cornerstone. In him the whole building is joined together and rises to become a hold temple in the Lord. And in him you too are being built together to become a dwelling in which God lives by his Spirit" Ephesians 2:14-22.

Being a white, middle-class American obviously limits my empathy and understanding of experiencing racial difficulties. Honestly, I can remember no instance in college, much less my lifetime, where the color of my skin affected the way I was treated. With that said, I will leave these stories to my precious brothers and sisters who have sadly had to experience the effects of racial prejudice. I long to grow in my love and understanding of these men and women, prayerfully considering their plight and trusting a sovereign Father who longs to unify our hearts.

MY SWEET SURPRISE

LAFAYETTE COLLEGE

When I arrived on campus my freshman year, nothing about it was comfortable. I had visited the school one time, though only for a couple of hours. My dorm room was the size of my old laundry room and my bags barely fit into the hallway. Not to mention the social and cultural shock of being at a new school. Here I was, a good ole' southern girl prancing in from Arkansas, suddenly thrown onto a campus full of Long Island accents, Yiddish words, and people of different racial and ethnic backgrounds I didn't even know existed. It was dramatically different than anything I had ever known. My biggest shock, however, was yet to come. I had rarely come into contact with people of a different race, religion or cultural ethnicity—much less lived with one!

I was unaware, on that rainy move-in day, that God had anything resembling a good surprise in store for me. I had never been friends with a black person, let alone lived with one, so I must admit, I was a bit scared in first meeting Michelle. When her friendly hand reached out to greet me, however, accompanied by her 60-watt smile, I experienced a peace only God can provide. I still remained clueless on the impact she would have in shaping my college experience. Michelle would be that special person who made my first semester at Lafayette feel comfortable when everyone and everything else made me feel lost. She was going to be one of my very best friends.

Our late night laughs and Krispy Kreme runs during "Friends" are some of my fondest memories of college. Midnight tennis, study sessions, or her teaching me how to "really" dance, are memories I know will stay with me forever.

It wasn't just these childish times of fun that brought Michelle and me so close. She was one of the few people at college whom I felt comfortable opening up to, whether it was about my faith, excitements, joys, or fears. She would listen intently and offer encouraging advice whenever necessary. Being one of the only Christian women I would meet that freshman year, Michelle was a special link to fellowship and shared communion with God. Our different backgrounds and experiences taught me so much about our God and His love for all people, races and nationalities.

I learned so much during my freshman year. I learned academically, but more importantly, I learned about life. I recognized that the stereotypes I'd grown up accepting as truth were merely deceptive lies of the world. Michelle (thankfully) broke every stereotype I had known about people of different races and backgrounds. It's painful for me to recall the shocking reactions friends from home had, in finding out that my college roommate was an African-American. I am even more humiliated to admit that I had had the same misconceptions just months earlier. Thankfully though, the Lord has used this experience in a powerful way, reminding me that not skin color, let alone anything else, can ever be too big for Him. God has fearfully and wonderfully made us, not that we might attain sameness, but that we might glorify Him in our oneness through Jesus Christ.

MIXING COLORS

MISSOURI STATE

I confess that I am writing this from a middle-class, Caucasian perspective, therefore immediately robbing me of much understanding and empathy to the cause. Honestly, I can remember no instance in college, much less my lifetime, when the color of my skin (with the exception of freckles maybe), affected the way I was treated. At the same time, however, I have seen the direct impact and destruction the

issue continues to create. Racial separation and even segregation remain a huge problem on campuses across this
nation. And Christian organizations are no strangers to
these problems.

If anyone were going to attempt to unify over skin
color and race, wouldn't it seem plausible to be the
Christians? Shouldn't we be the ones who love our neigh-
bors above ourselves and treat one another as sisters and
brothers in Christ? Well why is it that our churches and
ministries are often the most exclusive groups of any?

Why is it that our ministries are separated by
denomination, skin color, ethnicity and even social status?
Or more daunting than that, why is it that there might be a
black, white, Korean and Chinese Baptist church, all at the
same intersection? Nature and science reveal that we are
creatures of habit and certainly creatures who migrate to
those who resemble us. But there is exciting news for
Christians. Because of the death and resurrection of Jesus
Christ, we are now "united with Christ" (Philippians 2:1)
and "will make *his* joy complete by being like-minded, having the same love, being one in spirit and purpose" (verse 2).

I don't know where your campus ministry lies in this
discussion, or even how you personally relate to this issue,
but I do know one thing. God doesn't work through one
ethnicity or cater to one people group. Therefore, it's naive
and frankly, impossible, given the diversity of our nation
and campuses today, to think that a singularly faceted,
exclusive ministry could impact an entire campus. Rather,
through seeking a bond of unity, peace and grace through all
of the ministries, the body of Christ will unquestionably
function in its inherent capacity of beauty and miracles.

Is this practical? Hardly. But is this possible?
Absolutely! That is if we are willing to step out of our personal and collective comfort zones and passionately seek to

align our ministries with God and His pursuit of all students on our campuses. The best application of everything is always prayer.

The pressure we face to conform to society and it's ways of grouping are not going to disappear. As Christians, however, the capacity to overcome that disunity was born 2000 years ago at the cross. We are not called to forsake our uniqueness, but we are called into one body. Becoming a believer doesn't mean being stamped with a restricting mark of sameness, but rather a unique identity of redemption in Christ. And we should rejoice as students who can now minister together, "Therefore, since we have been justified through faith, we have peace with God through our Lord Jesus Christ, through whom we have gained access by faith into this grace in which we now stand. And we rejoice in the hope of the glory of God" (Romans 5:1-2).

A COMMON LANGUAGE

EMORY UNIVERSITY

As sad as it may be, Christian ministries are often the most segregated of any group on campus. Whether it's a separation of denominations, Greek vs. non-Greek, or athletes vs. intellectuals, skin color remains no exception. I thought it would be interesting to gain perspective from a ministry trying to combat these tendencies of segregation. In the interview below the same questions were presented to an African American woman (S: Shanetta) and a white woman (V: Vanessa), who were placed in the same discipleship group. The interviews were done on an individual and private basis, allowing the interviewees to be as honest as possible.

1) What was your first impression of being in a group with all whites (or with a black person)?

S: Being in an all-white group never really felt awkward, because I didn't grow up in a segregated environment. I was often the black person among a group, or team of whites. But I guess it's always a little weird at first, because you're looking, or hoping for that one person to connect with, in any new group. But for better or for worse, the feeling naturally subsided as usual. I have a lot of black friends, but I have a lot of white friends, too. I knew coming into the group that the thoughts and actions I would do in a group of whites would be a little different than if I were with blacks. That's not a bad thing, per se, just a cultural fact. We may all live in America, but there definitely remains a white and a black culture.

V: When I arrived at our first group meeting and saw there was a black girl, I was initially surprised. I remember feeling ashamed at the time and am even embarrassed now for expecting our small group to be all white. My first thoughts were that we weren't going to have a lot in common. I didn't put up a wall or look down on her, I was just mentally preparing myself that I may not be able to relate to Shanetta as well as the others. I tried to have an open mind, but for some reason part of my heart remained hesitant. At my church back home, we never had intimate groups mixing various races. It seemed like all the races were lobbying for "equality," and in doing so were always forming their own elite groups. It felt like we were all co-existing in our own separated organizations.

2) What presuppositions did having someone of another race create, in terms of your hopes for the group?

S: Because I didn't allow myself to focus on the fact that I was the only black in the group, I didn't feel uncomfortable being in public and just hanging out with any of the girls. But, I did realize early on that there were some things that differed and might never be understood in a group of whites, as it would in a group of blacks. For example, when I'm with my black friends, we might joke about the so-called "diversity" on our campus, knowing that it really doesn't exist, though always makes for a good brochure or published statistic. I'm not saying that my group would never understand this, among other issues, but there's just a certain comfort level that happens naturally when relating to my black friends.

V: When I pictured our small group, I imagined a group of girls so close knit that we shared our most intimate secrets with one another. But because of my own hesitations in getting to know Shanetta, my ideas of intimacy and closeness seemed to fade a bit. I still desired, however, to learn how to love this girl and try to relate to her as best that I could.

3) What have you been most challenged by in knowing Vanessa (or Shanetta)?

S: If by "challenged," you mean difficulty getting to know Vanessa because of racial differences, than there were honestly no challenges. I just looked at her as a friend, and really didn't see any challenges in the fact that we were two different races. I guess the biggest challenge for me has been sharing prayer requests for the economic hardships of my family. I don't like to make assumptions, but most whites that attend Emory come from families that have financial stability, and for some reason it's really hard for me to relay these personal requests. I know this is bad, but I almost feel like I'm inferior in some way, because I know Vanessa's never really "suffered" financially before. I hope it doesn't sound like I'm saying all blacks are poor, or even that I'm necessarily poor. But for some reason, this issue specifically, has consistently been a challenge for me to share with Vanessa, where as it would never be with a black friend. In all honesty though, the response I received from the first time I swallowed my pride and shared this burden, I was blown away by her compassionate and sympathetic heart.

V: I don't think *challenged* is quite the word I would use in describing Shanetta. Blessed is more like it. It has been amazing what God has taught me despite my immaturity in understanding racial relations. Although I have never been "prejudiced" in terms of viewing one culture as superior to another, my heart has always assumed that other races wouldn't understand me as well as my own. God has radically broken that assumption for me. Shanetta is one of the most amazing people I've ever met, and I have been overwhelmed by how much we have in common and how similar our hearts are. Looking back it makes sense, because if the Lord has made himself a home in both of our souls, then why shouldn't they connect in a supernatural way? I recognize the Jesus in her, and she recognizes the Jesus in me. It has been an awesome experience through which God has taught me that all of his children have the same fears, hopes, dreams, struggles, and even the same crazy sense of humor. I am blessed beyond measure in knowing Shanetta as my friend.

4) What have you been most amazed by in your relationship with Vanessa (or Shanetta)?

S: One thing that has really amazed me is that I can reach a comfort zone with Vanessa. That I don't have to feel like I'm inferior. She doesn't think differently about me when I tell her about my financial situation. Just because she's doesn't struggle with that issue, there are other things she struggles with. And I feel like I can use my struggles as testimonies to her, and she can do the same with me. We can encourage each other. God has created a strong bond between us, because I feel like she's not just "one of my white friends" (even though I would never refer to her that way), but she's simply my friend. She is my Christian friend who I can grow spiritually with, hang out and just plain have fun with.

V: I have been overwhelmed in talking with Shanetta about the Lord and doing morning Bible studies with her. It has been a great experience to affirm and challenge one another through God's Word. Her heart continues to amaze me in so many ways. Shanetta has a fervent love for His will and giving Him glory. It definitely validates the Word of God in my heart that across cultures, the language of prayer and adoration to our Savior remains constant. Praise God!

5) Has your friendship with Vanessa (Shanetta) changed your perspective of God in any way?

S: Most definitely. Vanessa has been such an encouragement to me. Her friendship has proven to me even more that God is a big God. He doesn't want us to limit our relationships to our comfort zone; He wants to spread the wealth and power of His name. Our friendship is like a witness to others, because they see that we are not tied down by skin color. I have always known that God is the God of all the earth, and has no limits or boundaries. And our friendship has further strengthened that in me. I feel such a boundless hunger for Christ, because I see that Vanessa has that same hunger. Despite our physical differences, we are sisters in Christ, passionately pursuing and living in the hope of meeting our Lord and Savior face to face.

V: My relationship with Shanetta has shown me that God is not one of confusion. Even though my life might be completely different from a young girl in China, or a woman in Russia, God speaks to hearts in the same way. When He comes into a life and draws a soul to himself, He impacts us in the same sweet way, no matter how different we are. It has been neat to see how although Shanetta and I came from incredibly different families, geographic locations, experiences and even church backgrounds, we have both maintained a common ground in Jesus Christ.

6) How do you foresee this friendship influencing your life and views of other races in the future?

S: This friendship will further confirm that friendship knows no limits. This is not my first non-black friend, and it will not be my last. I like making friends with other people besides blacks. The reassurance that everyone struggles and everyone has his or her fears and weaknesses is something I often forget. By increasing my circle of friends, Vanessa's relationship has expanded my concept of interconnectedness in the world. God continues to comfort me in seeing that I have so many places to turn for a helping hand, regardless of its color.

    V: I think it has allowed me to be more transparent with people of other races. My friendship with Shanetta is a beautiful gift from God, and one that I am glad my own ignorance did not cause me to miss out on. I think I'll be more open and honest now, realizing that God alone has the power to sew His people together. In knowing that we are all one body, I can only hope to be constantly mindful of remaining unified in Christ, that His kingdom might be furthered. Few people ever get to know someone as special as Shanetta, and I anxiously await the other people and other races that the Lord delicately weaves into my life.

A MIXED ME

SOUTHERN METHODIST UNIVERSITY

    For those of you who are bi-racial, I need not give an explanation as to what this word means. But for the rest of the population, being bi-racial means that each of your parents comes from a different ethnic background. The beauty of this word and concept, bi-racial, is that is can incorporate any ethnic group in God's wonderful earth.

There is a misconception that there are many different skin colors. In fact, there is only one, melanin. Having little melanin makes us light skinned and more melanin makes us darker skinned. And the natural conclusion is that people of varying melanin levels will produce unique offspring. The bi-racial issue comes in when the melanin levels are completely different.

    My hope in this reflection is to simply address the core issue and struggle that my being bi-racial causes on a daily basis. The United States is far from cleansed from the violent and hate-filled history that took place before, during and after our nation's Civil War. Today, the outward remains of that hatred are manifested as an inward, dichotomous mind-set. There are literally no two ethnic groups in the United States so separate in everyday life than blacks and whites.

Several bi-racial people have spoken out, either directly or indirectly, communicating their sole identity with being black. Now, please understand that I truly celebrate this choice. I honestly feel that it is their God-given right to choose how they want to identify themselves, but here is the problem: I don't identify myself that way. If there were ever a specially defined bi-racial ethnicity, I would claim that, for I do not claim to be black, or white, but both.

I was born in Kansas, raised in Florida and attend college in Atlanta. I attended a predominantly white elementary school, but my middle school had a better blend of various ethnicities. My high school was mainly black. Thus, I have been blessed with exposure to both cultures. Presently, I attend a University with Caucasians as the majority. I am a member of a black church, and am very involved with a mostly white on-campus fellowship. One of my roommates is black. The other two roommates are white, and I am attracted to many different types of guys. I tell you all of these facts so that you can get a glimpse of what being bi-racial means to me. It is often confusing, and everyday I catch myself thinking about how my bi-racial identity gets fleshed out in my life. It seems a consistent paradox that when my fellowship in either a predominantly white or black group begins to grow, increased feelings that I do not belong in either one tend to creep up. The most difficult emotional struggle I have is that I am part of both groups, but do not truly belong to either one, as if I am in no man's land or straddling the fence. In short, for awhile I felt like my effort to celebrate both of my heritages often left me feeling more isolated than anything else. Yet my desire is clearly to celebrate and accept both sides of me.

For me, I've realized that the healthiest way to approach my bi-racial identity is seeking friendships with Christians who are black and white. I don't mean fulfilling some sort of racial quota, but I do mean to continue my personal growth of what I believe being bi-racial means. Any person can grow in understanding that the Body of Christ holds no loyalty to a given skin color. In fact, praising God with various languages, ages and skin colors can be some of the most amazing worship you'll ever experience! In living a life set apart for our Creator, the most important factor is not the color of a person's skin, but the quality of a person's relationship to Jesus Christ. Thanks be to God.

In college, God has slowly been teaching me what it looks like to love Christians of all ethnicities, because in short, this is His heartbeat—relaying His love to all nations and nationalities and ethnicities. A common love and pursuit of Jesus Christ is a unity that can never be broken. I have discovered the biggest and most loving family in the entire world: the Body of Christ. In the Body, these issues tend to fade. They are pushed to the periphery as I realize my place in God's family, regardless of the circumstances or surroundings. My value lies in Christ and His Body alone. I realize that the love in His family is all sustaining and satisfying. I pray that God would continue to move me more into alignment with this focus, while simultaneously blessing me with rich cultural experiences drawing from both my ethnic backgrounds. All in all, my biggest revelation is simple: because I am a child of the Most High God, I am just like you, my brother, and you are just like me, my sister.

MY THOUGHTS ON RACISM

GORDON COLLEGE

My heart becomes angered at the thoughts and actions generated by racism. I did not grow up in an environment where blacks and whites were treated differently. The racism I learned was specific to Hispanics and Filipinos. Growing up in southern California forced me to think that diversity is fine, until it invades the supremacy of whites. I've never considered the reality of people's thoughts and subtle actions influencing my belief systems and specifically, my prejudices. As I look back, however, I realize how fortunate I am to have a decent understanding and respect for diversity, given that I was constantly surrounded by it.

The remaining threads of racism in our nation often fascinate me. More profoundly, however, is the way that the church, in many ways, fuels this racism. How is this possible? How can the ignorance of Christians be so harmful, yet I remain proud to call myself a follower of Christ? I am strikingly embarrassed at the ignorance of Christians, so why do I choose to associate myself with such people? Or do I? In praying through these questions, I realize that in noticing the stupidity of my fellow brothers and sisters, I too, am reminded of my sin and prejudice driven nature. This pushes me to question the sins in my life that entangle and disillusion me?

Recently, God's been teaching me about the need for the Church in our society. Prior to this, I was determined that Christ could more easily reveal His truth without the church and its hypocrisy. He doesn't need a group of people who claim one thing on Sunday, yet practice another throughout the week. And the short of it is, the church is simply a body of professed believers who rarely ever own up to sinning. But the fact of the matter is, Christ doesn't *need* any of us to change hearts or accomplish his work in and through the church. But he has *chosen* to use us for His glorious purposes.

Racism is clearly a sin. This doesn't need verification by a scripture, or a sermon. The pain and anguish that it causes in our hearts is proof enough. But something I struggle with is why everyone's heart doesn't seem pierced by this sin. In fact, my eyes shed tears at the thought of others not being compelled to combat this broken state of being. That others do not see the inherent anguish that burns within me when I hear a slanderous comment, or a degrading joke hurts deep down. My heart breaks in the process and my mind begins a game of tug-of-war with the possible actions that could be taken.

Today I think about my campus and even my body of fellowship, knowing that I have also lived in the sin of racism. Yet, I must rest in the knowledge of being freed from this sin by the cross of Christ, and able to rejoice in no longer tolerating its existence. It is not my wisdom, intelligence, or upbringing that opened my eyes to and cleansed me from a prejudiced heart. I am no different than another person. So my conclusion remains succinct; there must be a greater cause, a larger power, and a better reason. It is grace alone that lead my broken heart to repentance. Racism is a deadly virus that continues injecting diseases on campuses and campus ministries across our nation. It is only through clothing ourselves in the fitted gloves of grace that we, as Christians, can combat the malicious force of racism.

WE DON'T HAVE TO BE DIFFERENT

UNIVERSITY OF NORTH FLORIDA

Nadia was the nicest cafeteria lady I had ever met. There was never a day during my first two years of eating in the dining hall when her stunning Ethiopian face didn't radiate an enormous smile and aura of joy. From the start, we were friends, rarely talking about more than our weekend plans or an upcoming test, but nonetheless, God blessed us with a relationship that I looked forward to at every mealtime. Occasionally, we would share about our churches and faith. Though Nadia never pushed it too much, she often asked if I would like to attend her church. My immediate response was always no, given that I was very involved in a local church near my campus and couldn't imagine missing a Sunday.

After at least a year of dreaming up excuses for Nadia and for myself, I finally decided to take her up on the offer. In short, I will never view my faith, my race, Nadia, or myself in the same way after that experience. The entire congregation at her church was Ethiopian. I've been to a lot of churches, but confess that I was completely surprised by much that went on that morning. In fact, just about every one of my expectations was shattered. For one, the four-hour service was a lot longer than I'd expected.

Furthermore, the music was different, the building, the people, the procession, the pastor and the language was different! But there was something unbelievably comfortable and even unifying, making these tangible differences melt into a unique unison. I realized that morning how big the God we serve is. I had failed to recognize that my typical Sunday experience, my rituals, assumptions, expectations and priorities do not define *the way*. They are not *the truth* and they are not *the life*. I was reminded that morning that as much as my mouth claims it, my heart strays far from loving as if there is only *one way*. From breathing as if there is only *one truth*. And from living as if there is only *one life*, that of God the Father and His Son Jesus Christ. Far too often, it is my selfish and egocentric understandings that paint the face of God.

Spending time with Nadia that morning was a timeless investment, let alone a life changing experience. I was able to meet and interact with her family, as well as submit, for one morning, to her life and circumstances. For the first time in our relationship, there was no serving glass between us. The difference in our skin tones was flooded with something that made that colored barrier dissolve into nothing. I realized that morning that difference does not necessitate being different. Although Nadia's church didn't match the mold that I was accustomed to, nor did the rituals, skin color, or language of the congregation, her faith and reason for living pointed toward the same God that mine did. Nadia's heart cradles the word of God and her soul longs for the very fulfillment of Christ's love, just as mine does.

It seems a shame that we've let God's creativity of mankind become a stumbling block to the intended cohesive work of His body of Christ. The pigment of skin color is merely a shadow of what lies beneath. And the closer you get to the subject, the more alike each becomes. Mankind's hearts are incredibly similar. They all begin at one point and end at another, while beating pretty identically in the meantime.

God loves to be loved. In fact, He is love and created people to love Him. Thus, our hearts merely long to be loved. So whether it's a cafeteria worker, or anyone else, may we posture our lives in such a way that love becomes our cornerstone. Let's not love a given person, or a specific people group, or even the body of a sanctioned church. But may we love as God loves, not based on a difference, or a similarity. Instead, let's fall in love with the core of God's heart. In turn, we will fall in love with the identical core heart needs of His creation.

CHAPTER 11

GOD'S SURPRISE ENCOUNTERS

So do not fear, for I am with you; do not be dismayed, for I am your God. I will strengthen you and help you; I will uphold you with my righteous right hand.
Isaiah 41:10

I think one of God's greatest desires is to bless us daily with His rich love and affection. This may come through conversations, opportunities, or just pure beauty in nature. His plans are going to happen regardless, and His blessings will be unconditionally showered. But in praying for open eyes to see them, and in asking for open ears to hear them, I think the majestic nature of God's blessings becomes all the more real and powerful in our lives.

After class during my freshman year, a few of us were standing around talking about our plans for the weekend. After everyone had shared about exciting activities and events they had planned, the question came to me. I knew very well what I was doing that weekend, but the bottom line was, I was embarrassed to say it. I think the way I finally ended up wording it was, "I'm going on some retreat type thing with a bunch of friends." And of course right after I said this, I quickly diverted the attention back to everyone else's plans.

Yes, it was a retreat and yes, it was with a bunch of friends, but it was also an evangelism training conference (which I obviously needed). Solely by the grace of God, one of the guys in the conversation approached me after class and boldly ask, "Does the retreat happened to be

Christian?"

"Yes", I was now able to respond confidently. "You're not going too, are you?"

"No, but I had no idea there were other Christians on this campus, let alone a Christian organization that would plan a retreat."

Praise God for the courage of this sweet friend of mine, who is now very involved in our campus ministry. He reminded me of the beauty of not being ashamed of our amazing Savior. Joshua gives similar encouragement in verse 1:9, when he explains our command to "Be strong and courageous. Do not be terrified; do not be discouraged, for the Lord your God will be with you wherever you go." Learn from my mistake and speak up about the things God is doing in your life, for you never know who might be listening.

I JUST NEEDED TO ASK

UNIVERSITY OF CALIFORNIA, BERKELEY

My university is not one you might call "a Christian campus." Thus, it's not the easiest place to find solid Christian friends. My freshman year, apart from my roommate (completely God's grace) and two other students in my dorm, I knew no committed disciples of Christ. For me, this was a huge transition, coming from an incredible group of strong Christian friends at home. I kept waiting for God to send someone knocking on my door, but nothing happened. I finally concluded that this was the way it was supposed to be, and God must have intended for me to have no Christian companions.

About halfway through my sophomore year, I

changed my mind and decided this just couldn't be right. I really needed some Christian fellowship. I began praying more specifically and earnestly about this (ah ha, prayer as a solution to my troubles), but honestly, still held onto my doubts.

About a week after I'd started praying this prayer, I was out with some new sorority sisters. While driving home, one of the girls randomly asked if I knew of any campus Bible studies. I almost drove off the side of the road in shock; but instead, a bit startled, asked her somewhat defensively, "Why are you asking me? Who put you up to this?" I told her I didn't know of any Bible studies, but that I'd certainly be willing to start one! So we discussed the specifics and made plans to start an in-depth study of God's will for our daily lives. At first we planned on making it just the two of us, but of course when quietly discussing our plans at a sorority dinner one night, God perked up the ears of another girl, and proceeded to add her to our group. And by the end of our first week, a fourth girl had asked to join us.

A few months ago, I was convinced of being alone in my walk with Christ on this campus. After relinquishing my anxieties and loneliness to prayer, however, God brought me to several other girls searching for my same desires. This weekly fellowship and study of God's plan for our lives has made an enormous difference in my college life, as well as in my life with Christ. God has not only blessed me with new friends, but He's also blessed me with friends who share my pursuit and love for Him.

THE HAWK

RICE UNIVERSITY

On my way to class one day, something amazing happened. A majestic gray hawk swooped over my head, en route to its next perch. Simple, yet out-of-the-ordinary moments like this, remind me of the incredible joys God displays for us. I followed this hawk to its landing point, which ended up being about 50 yards ahead of me. I was truly blessed in watching this exotic creation view our campus from his lofty nest above. I looked at his piercing black eyes, created by God to allow his ability to see for miles and miles. What a great morning I had thinking and meditating on this unbelievable bird of prey.

In chapter 5 of Galatians, Paul teaches us about the fruit of the Spirit. Literally, they are the fruit of righteousness. So essentially, God experiences this fruit as well. One fruit of the spirit is joy. When I began thinking about how God could possibly experience joy, I was perplexed. Judging from the day-to-day activities of our lives, I didn't understand how God could possibly experience joy.

A very special friend of mine shared an analogy, through which God hit me with a powerful truth. When was the last time you surprised someone? And, who do you think experienced more joy from the surprise? When I surprise someone, I'm often so overly excited to see his or her reaction, that I don't even keep it a surprise! That's it! Do you understand? Can you picture God, standing on the edge of heaven, almost eager about seeing us experience His surprises. Wow! And I'm convinced that God's joy doesn't just come from the "big surprises," but also from the seemingly little blessings that we too often consider mere coincidence.

Can you imagine God watching as that hawk flew over my head? Can you see Him laughing, as I jumped with surprise, and then contently watching me enjoy my time gazing upon the bird. Do you remember the last time God gave you a surprise like that? I'm learning that whether we recognize them, or not, they happen every day.

Maybe you are going through a difficult time in your walk with Christ, but just imagine God, sitting upon His throne and almost getting "giddy" over the surprises He has in store for you. Hang in there, because I have a hunch that today He has a surprise blessing with your name written on it.

He Was Tempted Too

James Madison University

It's tempting to imagine God as a saintly, old man, sitting on some golden throne, or maybe even a full-size rocking chair, answering prayers and keeping the world on its proper axis. The amazing thing though, is that our God is about the farthest thing from old and is definitely not boring or outdated. In fact, our God is the inventor of creativity, the leader of ingenuity and the lover of progression. Our lives are a reflection of His image – we are created with the utmost precision and creativity. You don't have to go far to embark upon creativity beyond our wildest dreams.

Try to explain the intricacy of a flower. Describe the making of a sunrise. Imagine the delicacies of a child's birth. Furthermore, the term complexity doesn't begin to explain our minds. And our hearts are on an ongoing journey of progression, being perfected in the image of God and carried to completion until the day Christ returns. In short, our God is the hippest, most humorous, uncontainable brilliant and passionate lover of life. He is amazing.

Our God is not a wallflower, or a "let's stay at home and pray for the diseased and the unloved." He is a peace-making pursuer of hearts, who willfully chooses to help the helpless and to love the loveless. And He uses us as His ambassadors!

We know from experience that serving God doesn't come without challenged motives and intentions. It doesn't always happen without pressure and temptation too. But we weren't called to fear pressure or never enter a situation that might allow temptation. Rather, we were called to be grounded and strengthened by the mighty hand of God, that we could endure and persevere through these situations, ultimately glorifying the power of His name.

And the writer of Hebrews assuredly writes that, "For we do not have a high priest who is unable to sympathize with our weaknesses, but we have one who has been tempted in every way, just as we are—yet was without sin. Let us then approach the throne of grace with confidence, so that we may receive mercy and find grace to help us in our time of need" (Hebrews 4:15-16).

This verse implies a lot of things, but one that stands out to me is that we are going to be tempted. College is no exception to this rule. In fact, it could quite possibly be one of the most tempting times of your life. As Christians, it's easy for us to think we are above temptation, or can avoid it by remaining in our enclaves of good, little Christian friends. But these verses do not specify any of the above remarks. Rather, they claim that Christ himself was tested and willingly faced the trials of temptation. Our Savior is personal and intimately concerned about relating and connecting with us on every possible level. Jesus cares about the struggles that you and I endure. He's not ashamed when we fail. He doesn't turn His back when we stumble. But He sympathizes with our pain and He cries with our sorrows. It is the care of Christ that stands as our refuge, and it is His kindness that gently leads us to repentance.

Another incredible truth from these verses is the very concept of our ability to "approach the throne of grace with confidence," because of these attributes of Jesus. When he endured incredible temptation from Satan, He boldly sought the Word of God in receiving mercy and grace in His time of need (Luke 4:1-13). We have been entrusted with this living and active power that is sharper than any double-edged sword (Hebrews 4:12). The Word of God is our sustaining breath in life, let alone during times of weakness. And it is for this reason that we can have confidence during a trial (at a fraternity party, in a relationship, or during that un-proctored exam). God didn't call us to live sinless lives in college. He knows we're incapable of that. But He did send us a sinless Savior, who sacrificed His life for you and for me, so that our temptation and weakness would not be feared and avoided. Through Christ's life, we have the strength to confidently walk out on the limb, gathering the fruit that God has prepared for us. And we can boldly face the suffering and endure the darkness in our lives, so that the abounding love and life of Christ will reign in us, as we turn and face the shining light.

LOLLIPOPS

SAMFORD COLLEGE

I don't suck my lollipops. When it enters my hand, I practically tear it open and bite right to its core. But I have no idea why. So I started thinking about this one day and came up with the following: all I want is the instant burst of flavor. I definitely get that flavor, but when I look around,

15 minutes after my lollipop is long gone, others are still savoring and enjoying theirs.

Does the way we eat lollipops describe the relationship so many of us have with our Heavenly Father? Often, all we desire from God is that sudden burst of "flavor." We wander around, waiting for that high of emotional feelings inside of us. And I think it's typical to see those "stronger" Christians and wonder how they possibly do it. How can their walks not be based on emotional highs? My conclusion is they do it by maintaining a daily relationship with God. They don't live for a fuzzy feeling here, or goose bumps there, but a constant and continual desire to know and follow God. They don't bite into their suckers. They *savor* every minute they get to spend with it.

Some of my biggest mistakes in college have come from impulsively biting into various lollipops. When one sucker was gone, I realized my need to find another, often bigger and better than the first. Essentially, what began as an alluring pleasure, even a spiritual high, quickly became an empty stick—leaving me neither nourished, nor sustained. In doing this time after time, I have said and done many things I now regret. More crucial, however, I have lost many nourishing and sustaining opportunities with God. Oh Lord, how I want to savor my lollipops, and most importantly, how I want to savor You.

MARY OR MARTHA

COLORADO UNIVERSITY

A warm April evening in Boulder, Colorado, is arguably one of the most perfect settings in the world. As I sat out on our campus quad, reflecting on the hopes and dreams from four years behind me, I had one of those "God moments." I had read a quote earlier that morning that never left my mind. Author Philip Yancey said, "There is nothing we can do to make God love us more and there is nothing we can do to make God love us less." The echo of these words was accompanied by an incredible peace, but also by an uncanny sense of regret. If I had grasped any sense of the meaning of this quote before the final days of college, I can't imagine how my years would have been different.

Remember the story in Luke 10:38-42? Basically Christ was invited into the home of two women, Mary and Martha. Mary chose to sit at the feet of Christ, while Martha worked endlessly making preparations in their home. Distracted by all the work she felt Mary had left her, Martha came pleading to Jesus, asking how this possibly seemed fair. "Martha, Martha," the Lord answered, "you are worried and upset about many things, but only one thing is needed. Mary has chosen what is better, and it will not be taken away from her."

I can't tell you how much I related to Martha during college. I was a "doer." In fact, I still am a "doer." Every day of my life calls me to question: Do I live out the Martha path, or rest in the role of Mary. Don't get me wrong, serving is great, but there is a call to surrender before there is a call to service. I distracted myself with numerous ministries, clubs, organizations and teams. My schedule was busy, but I had always thrived on this lifestyle. And moreover, I knew that serving God was my passion, so what better way to do this than all over campus? Well, that night on the quad, quite a few thoughts came to mind.

For one thing, my service to God often turned into a disservice to me. I would neglect my times alone with the Lord in order to spend time serving someone else.

Unfortunately, however, it's impossible for us to truly serve and love someone else when we're depending solely on ourselves. There's only one source for that ability, God. Therefore, I not only found myself tired and worn down much of the time, but I was also never able to go beyond my limited strength and tap into the unlimited strength of God.

Second, my role as Martha formed a stark separation between God and me. I was always so busy working *my* miracles and planning *my* path, that I often lost sight of the cross of Jesus Christ. I lost sight of the fact that my Savior had come down from heaven, that I might die to myself and gain life into Him. I had lost sight of the fact that it wasn't up to me to change the world, let alone my campus. Rather, it was up to my surrender at the foot of the cross.

I praise God for Martha and her servant heart. But I also praise God for Mary and her recognition and awe of Christ. I praise Him that Mary saw the richness of what it means to have relationship with Jesus—to gladly rest at His feet and listen to His words. I hope I will always have a heart for service, but I hope that above that, I will have a restful and undistracted heart, knowing that my ability to serve God's kingdom is only possible through the work of the cross and my surrender to its beauty.

A Leap into Manhood

Elon University

There I was, standing on an overlook of a cliff, darkness surrounding me and my knees wobbling with fear. It was a warm summer night, yet my toes felt cold on the wet rocks that supported my nearly naked body. There was a feeling of uneasiness and excitement that swept through my mind, as it often does when I encounter uncertainty. I'm usually not one to unknowingly follow someone else's lead; I need to know where we are going and the precise details of the trip at hand. And in this particular situation, everything that had been planned had failed; yet I was on the brink of an unexpected discovery and wild realization about my personhood.

I had been studying the intention God had in creating men to be wild and adventurous. I found myself measuring these thoughts on the backdrop of my childhood and everything my mother had engrained in me. This was a new and deeply challenging outlook for me. I found that these longings for adventure were precisely what my inner desires cried out for, yet I'd never been able to explain. I longed to be freed from suburban living, trapped in concrete. I was tired of the distractions and facades that Americans are so good at hiding themselves behind. And finally, I was just fed up with my suppressed heart, tired of denying the very adventures and excitement that God created me to experience. As I fearfully anticipated my jump off the cliff that night, the culmination of my emotions started me on a discovery that God had made me like Himself: passionate, adventurous and wild with desire to rescue and free others. The feelings that roared like a lion from the depths of my soul were hard to articulate.

As the rest of my small group debriefed later that night, we found that all of us had felt humbled by God's unique, yet very similar teaching to each of our hearts. We realized that as brothers in the body of Christ, deep within our souls we had been created with an incredible similarity; we were all men of God, claimed and called His own. I understand that manhood is not something to be exalted, but it is an incredible birthright that I am slowly learning to embrace. Each gender maintains an incredible connection that moves beyond the explanation of words.

There was something about that night that made me realize that I was free and wild. It was more than a step into adulthood; it was a rite of passage within my inner being that describes who I really am in the eyes of God. I jumped from the ledge that night, not knowing or seeing my destination, but only judging my descent by the faint glare of reflection from the stars above. And as gravity took over, I began to fall to a mysterious place; my heart screamed.

Within seconds warm water saturated every crevice of my body. I opened my eyes to see complete darkness. As I floated upward, I took my first breath as a new man. I had discovered myself in the eyes of my Maker. It's interesting to ponder the timing of God. He chose a spontaneous, late summer night to reveal His glorious purposes in a magnificent way. It was at that rock quarry, a place I'd never before been to or heard of, that God chose to reveal to me that it was okay and even intentional for me to be wild within.

CHAPTER 12

SO YOU CAN DO IT!

If the Lord delights in a man's way,
he makes his steps firm;
though he stumble, he will not fall,
for the Lord upholds him with his hand.
Psalm 37:23

Society obviously has expectations for our college careers. And a lot of times, our parents, friends and professors do too. But I'm convinced that God also has expectations and hopes for our growth during these years. Hopefully this book has shown us clearly that yes, it is definitely possible to begin, maintain and strengthen your walk with God while in college. As we have read through these stories and may have already experienced in our own lives, this is by no means an easy task. God is going to teach us, test us, mold us and make us. But most of all, He's going to love us! I can guarantee that college will bring many ups and downs; but through it all, I can also guarantee that God will stand by us every step of the way! No matter what we've been through, are going through, or will go through in the days to come, take comfort in the words of Jeremiah 29:11 when God says, "For I know the plans I have for you," declares the Lord, "plans to prosper you and not harm you, plans to give you hope and a future."

Just think of what Jesus did to impact our world in a mere three-year time span of ministry. And He did this alone (I guess He had the Father and the Holy Spirit on his side, too). As Christians, we embody the very life and power of Jesus Christ, through His death and resurrection. Furthermore, He has "blessed us with every spiritual blessing in the heavenly realms" (Ephesians 1:3); so just imagine what God can do in and through us during these college years! Let's walk His path. Run His race. God has placed us, specifically, on our campuses with an awesome plan and purpose in mind. One of the most exciting things is that His hopes and dreams surely surpass any of the greatest of those we could ever imagine. God wants to out-do our wildest dreams. Let's love Him and have mighty hopes in Him. And as we take risks and step out of our comfort zones, let's trust God in providing and allowing for college to be some of the best years of our lives.